Guided Meditations for Children

How to Teach Children to Pray Using Scripture

Jane Reehorst, B.V.M.

Religious Education Division
Wm. C. Brown Company Publishers
Dubuque, Iowa

Table of Contents

Foreword:

Teaching Children to Pray Using Scripture

The form of meditation presented in this book is a successful means to teach children HOW to pray.

Using active imagination children are led into a Gospel scene where they are able to encounter the Lord Jesus. This approach to prayer has been used in the Church for centuries.

The scripture meditation process presented here can be incorporated into any Religious Education Series, either as an introduction or a conclusion to a Unit or a Lesson.

For those using the Light of Faith series from Wm. C. Brown Company, the meditations can often be incorporated into that step within the lesson plan called, "Proclaiming the Good News." As an alternative to having the children recall and reflect, the catechist can lead them in a meditation.

It is most important that the teacher participate in the meditation as it is being presented to the children. In order to do this effectively it is suggested that prior to the presentation the teacher spend some time meditating on the Gospel to be presented, becoming comfortable with this prayer form.

After personal reflection on the meditation, catechists may find that it would be helpful to tailor the meditation to better fit the needs of their children. Catechists working with young children, for example, may want to shorten the meditation or rephrase it occasionally to better suit the children's attention span or vocabulary. The goal is to teach the children *how* to pray and to make prayer an important part of their lives.

This book enables teachers or parents to help children learn a process for prayer. Each chapter in the book contains a meditation built upon a Gospel scene. Appropriate themes for each meditation can be found in the table of contents.

The process for each meditation is outlined in detail. Teachers and parents have only to review the meditation so that they can be comfortable with it. Read slowly, with a slight pause where indicated (. . . .). It is important to establish the appropriate atmosphere to enable the class to particpate fully in the meditation. If some children feel like talking or giggling, suggest that they take a few minutes to compose themselves. Allowing children to choose a position in which to pray will establish commitment on the part of the student and lead to greater comfort and relaxation. Give them the choice of sitting or lying on the floor or remaining in their seats.

After the meditation there is a silent time, no longer than one minute.

Do not be discouraged if at first the class does not pray spontaneously. Allow time to build a trust. Encourage them to say "Thank you, Lord," by asking if anyone would like to thank Jesus.

It is recommended that at the beginning of the year the teacher start with the meditation, "Meeting Jesus." This establishes a place in their imagination to meet Jesus at any time. Throughout the year prayer can be introduced by saying, "Let us go to our place to meet Jesus." Encourage the class to go there whenever they wish.

It is also recommended that each child in the class use a special notebook during meditation. This notebook will be used as a journal to record children's individual responses to their encounter with Jesus.

The various aspects of each chapter need no explanation. There is only one rule: keep it simple. Teaching children how to come to the Lord will not only affect you and your class now, but will lead children into a life long habit of effective prayer—the heart of Religious Education.

Acknowledgements

I wish to thank my family and friends who encouraged and supported me during the process of writing this book. I want to especially mention my close friend, Evelyn Salturelli, who not only supported me but helped edit this book; my friend, Father Jim Short, who encouraged me to write this book and helped edit; and to Sandy Hirstein who believed in what I was doing and enthusiastically supported me.

Meeting Jesus

John 20:11-18

Introduction

Sometimes I find it hard to talk to Jesus because I can't see him. Does anyone else have that problem? (Give the class time to respond.) There is a way to see Jesus. It is through our imagination. When you use your imagination, do you see people, places or things in your mind? (Give the class time to respond.) Using your imagination is one way we can see Jesus. I am going to bring you to a place where I meet Jesus. You may wish to go to another place, your favorite place. Do you have a special place? Why is it special to you? (It is important to allow a short time for discussion. It will give children time to recall special places in their lives.) As I describe my special place, you may imagine your special place.

Meditation

Close your eyes. . . . Take a deep breath . . . and relax. . . . There is a garden, . . . a special garden. . . . It is the place where Mary of Magdala was looking for Jesus after his resurrection. . . . Walk into this garden. . . . Feel the cool soft grass tickle your feet as you walk. . . . There are many beautiful shade trees here. . . . Some are tall and straight and have yellow green leaves. . . . There is a tree with a twisted trunk. . . . Its branches are close to the ground. . . . Some branches look strong enough to sit on. . . . Walk over to the tree and get out of the hot sun. . . . Sit on one of the branches. . . . You feel cool in the shade . . . and relief from the hot sun. . . . If you sit very quietly you can feel a gentle breeze on your face. . . .

Make yourself comfortable and look around the garden. . . . It is filled with color. . . . Look at all the flowers . . . pink and purple ones . . . white lilies . . . yellow daisies . . . and orange and red roses. . . . Breathe in deeply. . . . Smell the sweetness of all these flowers. . . . Notice all the birds. . . . Listen to them sing. . . . Some are chirping to each other. . . . There is another sound. . . . It is the gurgling of water. . . . There must be a creek nearby. . . . The sound is coming from behind some bushes filled with large red flowers. . . . Walk over and look for the creek. . . . It looks cool and refreshing doesn't it? . . . Listen to its gurgling sound. . . . Stoop down and put your hand in the creek. . . . Feel the cold water flow over your hand. . . . The creek is so clear that you can see the colorful smooth stones on the bottom. . . .

Someone is standing behind you. . . . Turn around and see who it is. . . . Feel your heart leap when you see that it is Jesus. . . . He smiles at you, . . . calls you by name, . . . and reaches out his hand to help you up. . . . Jesus hugs you. . . . Feel his hair and beard tickle your face. . . . His arms around you feel strong and protective don't they? . . . "Come," Jesus tells you. . . and he places his arm around your shoulders and leads you to a large tree beside the creek. . . . Sit under the tree next to Jesus. . . . Feel how good it is to be here with him. . . just Jesus and you . . . alone . . . together. . . .

What would you like to say to Jesus? . . . I am now going to give you a silent time so that you can talk . . . listen . . . or just be with him. (Allow about one minute of silence. Watch for signs of restlessness. If this happens before the minute is up, close the meditation.)

Closing Prayer (teacher lead)

It is time to leave you, Jesus. Thank you for being with me. I love you and will come back soon to be with you.

Say good-bye to Jesus. . . . Get up and begin to walk away. . . . Turn and wave. . . . Jesus smiles and waves back. . . . Open your eyes and come back into the room.

Sharing Time

Were you able to be in your special place? Did you like being with Jesus? What did you like best? Was it easier to talk to Jesus when you saw him in your imagination? Did you want to stay? Would you like to go there again? You can return any time you wish.

Follow-up

Purpose: Recreating the scene in which the child met Jesus will make it more vivid in the imagination. Provide each child with a piece of special paper (construction paper or drawing paper) because the picture is special. Choose one of the following activities.

1. Each child may draw and color the scene.
2. Each child may cut pictures out of magazines (trees, mountains, or beautiful colors) to create the scene.
3. Each child may draw, color and use magazine pictures to create their scene.

Find a picture of Jesus to paste on the scene in a favorite place.

Encourage the class to take the picture home and hang it up in their bedroom. (Some may wish to hang their picture in another place where the family can see it. Encourage this witness to the family.)

Always begin your class prayer time by inviting the children to go to their special place to be with Jesus. Allow a second or two for this.

Music

"By Name I Have Called You" from *By Name I Have Called You* (North American Liturgy Resources).

"Awaken! Come Alive" and "Color the World with Song" from *Young People's Glory and Praise* (North American Liturgy Resourses).

One Starry Night in Bethlehem

Luke 2:1–16

Introduction

(**Note:** It is important to keep the discussion short. The class will be inclined to become too involved with the subject of "birthdays.") Birthdays are exciting aren't they? Do you look forward to your birthday? What special things happen to you on that day? Does you mother or your father tell you about the day you were born? There is one birthday that everyone talks about. Whose birthday is it? Why does everyone think it is special?

Mary and Joseph must have been very excited about the coming birth of their baby. Joseph probably made a special baby crib. Mary probably spent time making baby clothes.

However, something happened to upset their plans. The Roman Emperor, Caesar Augustus, ordered that a census be taken of the entire Roman Empire. Everyone had to go to their hometown to register their name, so that they could be counted. Mary and Joseph had to travel a great distance on foot to their hometown of Bethlehem. And it was not a good time for Mary to travel, for she was about to give birth. But they had to obey the emperor's order.

Meditation

We are going to be with Mary and Joseph as they arrive in Bethlehem. . . . Close your eyes. . . . Take a deep breath . . . and relax. . . . It is evening, and you are in the overcrowded town of Bethlehem.

Joseph is leading a donkey through the streets. . . . Mary is seated on the donkey. . . . It has been a long, hard journey for them and they are very tired. . . . Mary is exhausted from riding the donkey because her baby is expected soon. . . . Joseph is looking for a place to sleep. . . . But he has not been able to find a place. . . . You are standing with Joseph and Mary in front of the last place to look. . . . Joseph sighs, . . . looks at the inn, or motel, . . . and asks you to hold the donkey's reins while he goes to talk to the manager of the inn. . . . Take the reins from Joseph. . . . It is hard to keep the donkey still . . . because people are pushing and shoving and often bump up against you and the donkey. . . . Mary is very quiet. . . . Turn to see if she is all right. . . . She is biting her lower lip in pain. . . . You realize that her birth pains have started. . .and wish Joseph would hurry. . . .

"He is coming" Mary whispers to you. . . . Joseph is hurrying toward you. . . . A maid from the inn is with him. . . . Her face is filled with concern as she walks up to Mary. . . . "There is no room in the inn," she tells Mary. . . . Feel your heart sink. . . . What will be done now?. . . . Joseph places his hand on Mary's arm and tells her that the maid will take them to a cave just outside of town. . . . "It will be warm. . .and we will have privacy," Joseph says. . . . Mary's face tightens in a quick pain. . . . "Please hurry Joseph, our baby is about to be born," she whispers. . . .

The maid from the inn quickly takes the donkey's reins from your hand. . . . "Help me make a way through this crowded street," she tells you. . . . Joseph walks beside the donkey and holds Mary's hand. . . . It is hard to push your way through the crowd . . . it almost seems impossible at times. . . . Somehow you find yourself outside the town and walking toward a nearby cave. . . . At the entrance the maid tells you to follow her . . . she lights a lantern that is in the cave. . . . "Help me make a bed of fresh hay," she orders. . . . Joseph is leading Mary into the cave . . . it is hard for her to walk. . . . He helps her lie down on the fresh hay bed you just helped make. . . .

Joseph asks you to wait at the entrance of the cave and pray for Mary. . . . As you pray, feel God's love and protection surround you. . . . In your heart you know that God is taking care of everything. . . . With Him all is well. . . . A baby's cry comes from inside the cave. . . . You wait. . . . Your prayers now turn to thanking God. . . . In a short time, the maid comes to you smiling. . . . "Mary has a fine healthy son," she tells you. . . . She steps back and allows you to enter the cave. . . .

Mary lies on the bed of hay. . . . The baby Jesus is in her arms. . . . She looks tired but happy and peaceful. . . . A bright smile lights her face as she looks at her baby and gently rubs his tiny fingers that rest in her hand. . . . There are tears of happiness in her eyes as she looks up and smiles at you. . . . Joseph is seated next to Mary. . . . His hand is gently stroking Mary's head. . . . "Isn't he beautiful?" Mary says. . . . Joseph smiles, . . . nods his head, . . .and with his finger gently strokes the baby's cheek. . . . Mary closes her eyes and seems to be asleep. . . . You and Joseph watch Mary and her baby. . . .

Later, Mary opens her eyes and looks at you. . . . "Would you like to hold Jesus?" she asks you. . . . You want to, . . .but you hesitate, for Jesus is so tiny, . . . you are afraid you might hurt him. . . . Joseph seems to understand how you feel. . . . "Come, sit close to me and I will show you how to hold Jesus.". . . He gently takes Jesus from Mary's arms. . . . There is a warm glow on Joseph's face as he looks down at the baby cradled in his arms. . . . Joseph carefully places Jesus in your arms. . . . Feel a peace and joy flow through you as you hold Jesus. . . . What do you want to say to Jesus? . . . to Mary? . . . to Joseph?

I will leave you in silence so that you can be with Jesus, Mary and Joseph. . . .

Prayer

I love you, Jesus. Thank you for coming into this world in order to save me. . . . Thank you for loving me enough to do this. . . . I believe that you are the Son of God. . . . Thank you, Mary, for saying "yes" when God asked you to be the mother of his Son. Thank you, Joseph for taking care of Jesus and Mary. (Invite spontaneous prayer.)

Journal Writing

Ask Jesus to help you express your thoughts and feelings as you write in your journal. Would you like to write a prayer of love and thanksgiving? Write what comes to your mind.

Sharing

Would anyone like to share their experience with the class? What is the most important gift you can give to Jesus? (themselves) How can you go about giving this gift to him? How can you bring Jesus to others? (Write their suggestions on the board. Lead them to include the insignificant things. . .smiling at someone, saying hello, listening when they would rather play; and spending a few minutes each night talking (praying) to Jesus and praying for others.)

Follow-up

Explain the following to the class. On Christmas Day we not only like to receive presents but also like to experience the joy of giving presents. It is important that we see the gift we give to someone. We also need to see the present we give to Jesus. Therefore, we are going to keep a record of our acts of kindness and prayers for others. Then on Christmas we well see for ourselves the gift we have given to Jesus. With each kind act we do and with each prayer we say for someone, we will make a flame. (Pass out a one inch pattern of a flame.)

On the flame the children will write the name of the person they prayed for or were kind to. They will thread the flame and make a large loop so that on Christmas Eve they can hang their flames on the Christmas tree or paste them in a decorated booklet to be placed under the tree or near the crib.

Closing Prayer

The class gathers around the Bible and the empty crib. The lights should be dimmed. Invite the class to go to the cave once again. Give them a second or two of silence for this.

Music

"Silent Night," "Oh, Little Town of Bethlehem."

"Children Run Joyfully," "Come, Lord Jesus," and "Violet in the Snow" from *Young People's Glory and Praise* (NALR).

Celebrating with Jesus at Cana

John 2:1–12

Introduction

Who can name special occasions when we take time out to celebrate? (List those given in a column on the board.) Why do we celebrate at these times? (List the reasons next to the occasions.) What special things do you do on these days? Do you think it is important to celebrate? Why?

Jesus enjoyed a celebration. We are going to be with him as he helps celebrate a wedding at Cana.

Meditation

Close your eyes. . . . Take a deep breath . . . and relax. . . . You are walking with Jesus and his disciples. . . . The disciples are laughing and joking . . . because they are looking forward to having a good time at a wedding feast in Cana. . . . Peter is telling everyone that he is planning on stuffing himself with all the good food he expects to find at the feast. . . . He laughs and pats his stomach. . . . John begins to tease him. . . . "Careful Peter, if you eat too much you won't be able to follow Jesus.". . . Peter stops laughing, . . . raises his eyebrows and asks why. . . . John places his hand on Jesus' shoulder, . . . winks at Jesus, . . . and turns to Peter. . . . "You know how Jesus loves to walk. . . . You won't be able to keep up with him, because you'll only be able to waddle around like a duck.". . . Everyone bursts out laughing and begins to tease Peter. . . . Jesus joins in. . . "Oh, I don't know about that, John, . . . we can always build a wagon large enough to hold Peter . . . and pull him around after us.". . . There is more laughter and more teasing. . . .

"Listen," James exclaims, "we must be nearing the house. . . . I can hear music and laughter.". . . Jesus, the disciples, and you all quicken your pace and soon the house is in sight. . . . Andrew begins to skip and clap his hands in time to the folk music and hurries ahead. . . . Some of the guests come down the path to meet you. . . . They all talk at once . . . welcoming you and telling you what has been happening at the celebration. . . . Mary hurries up to greet Jesus. . . . Turning to you she takes your hand and says. . . . "I'm so glad you were able to come.". . .

Reaching the house there are more greetings and more introductions. . . . In fact, there are so many you can't remember one name from the other. . . . Someone takes your arm and leads you to a table covered with food. . . . Peter has already found the table and is filling his plate with chicken, salads, fruit and fresh bread. . . . There is a twinkle in his eye as he looks your way. . . . As the other disciples join you, . . . you look for Jesus, . . . but he is nowhere to be seen. . . . A servant sets a pitcher of wine on the table. . . . He apologizes for the delay. . . . "For awhile we thought we ran out of wine, but we now have plenty.". . . Peter takes a sip. . . . "Best wine I've tasted in a long time," he comments as he wipes his mouth with his sleeve. . . .

The day seems to speed by and before you know it the sun is beginning to set. . . . Jesus walks up to you. . . . "Did you ever see a more magnificent sky?" he comments. . . . "Let's walk out into the field for a better view," Jesus says. . . . The setting sun seems to have painted the field gold. . . . "There isn't a green tree around," Jesus exclaims, "all of nature has turned into gold from the sun.". . . Jesus and you walk along silently. . . .

"All this splendor is free," Jesus tells you as he sweeps his arms out to embrace the scene before you. . . . "It is my Father's gift to us," he half whispers. . . . Turning to you, he makes a challenge. . . . "Let's see who can name the most gifts that now surround us.". . . You are about to begin, but Jesus stops you. . . . "In fact, let's make it a game. . . . Each gift we name is a point. . . . We'll even go beyond what we see here, we'll take in all of nature . . . and" . . . Jesus pauses, . . . looks at you and questions, . . ."Would you like to play this game?". . . "Oh yes, Jesus," you answer. . . . "Well, then let's start with the things of nature, . . .then the gift of people in our lives, . . . and if we have time, things made by people: . . . wine, chairs, toys, and so on. . . ." Jesus places his arms around your shoulders, . . .smiles radiantly at you and says, . . ."You know, we'll be celebrating my Father's gifts to us long after this wedding celebration is over. . . . Jesus stops, . . . turns to you. . .and says. . ."I'll let you begin the game.". . .

I'll leave you alone with Jesus to begin your game of celebration.

Prayer

Thank you, Father, for the gifts you have given us: . . . for the variety and colors of nature, . . . for the beautiful people you have sent into my life. . . . Thank you for surrounding me with all your gifts of love. (Invite spontaneous prayer.)

It is time to leave. . . . Say good-bye to Jesus . . . and begin to walk away. . . . Open your eyes and come back into the room. . . .

Journal

Continue the game you started with Jesus. Write down all the gifts that you can think of, especially those that are important to you. Ask Jesus to help you.

Sharing

What are some of the gifts that you listed in your journal? To celebrate means to praise someone like we do on national holidays. Look at the list on the board. Do we have a reason to celebrate?

Instead of giving speeches praising God, like they do for famous people on national holidays, let's make a mural. It will be our way of praising and thanking God for all His gifts that surround us.

Follow-up

(Before class prepare a long sheet of shelf paper by halfing the width. Stacks of magazines and glue should also be available.)

Invite someone to print in large letters across the mural "THANK YOU GOD FOR ALL YOUR GIFTS."

The children should begin the mural today and continue working on it for the next few weeks. This will give them time to collect pictures of family, friends, pets, etc. to paste on the mural. (Suggest that they select pictures of people working, praying, playing and eating together; receiving the sacraments, etc., besides pictures of nature. This mural would be a good offering to present at the preparation of gifts for the Thanksgiving Liturgy.)

Closing Prayer

Gather around the Bible and a candle. The teacher asks, "Did we mention the gift of each other in class?" To express this have them give each other a handshake of peace. Close by joining hands and singing.

Music

"Celebrate God" and "Glory and Praise to Our God" from *Young People's Glory and Praise* (NALR).

At the Jordan River with Jesus

Matthew 3:13-16; Mark 1:9-11; Luke 3:21-22

Introduction

Why is it important for us to feel that we belong to someone or to someplace? Let's make a list on the board of the places and people we belong to. How did we come to belong to these people and places? Are there people in the world who do not seem to belong anywhere? Who are they? How would you feel if you were in their circumstances? Why? Jesus knew that it is important to belong. We are going to be with him as he makes his choice to belong.

Meditation

Close your eyes. . . . Take a deep breath . . . and relax. . . . You are walking with Jesus on a journey from his home in Nazareth to Judea. . . . Jesus is leaving his home for the first time . . . and is about to start his mission. . . . You are making your way along a road in the Jordan Valley. . . . It is not the rich valley filled with grass, fields, flowers and trees that you expected. . . . Rather, it is filled with dense thickets and underbrush. . .and the trees are small. . . . There are some flowers that Jesus points out to you, . . . but not the kind you expected. . . . Jesus laughs,. . ."Farther down it will become even more dry and barren, . . . but there is beauty here if you look for it.". . .

"Where are we going, Jesus?" you ask. . . . "We are going to see my cousin, John. . . . He's now called the 'Baptist.' ". . . Jesus points to a large crowd gathered farther down the Jordan River. . . . "In fact, we are almost there. . . . See? . . . Those people are gathering around John to be baptized.". . .

"There he is," Jesus tells you as he points to a man standing in the middle of the river. . . . He is wearing an animal's skin tied with a rope for a belt. . . . People are wading up to him, . . . bowing their heads, . . . and allowing him to pour water over their heads. . . . "Why are people doing that?" you ask. . . . "They want to change," Jesus responds. . . . "By allowing John to baptize them, they are opening their hearts to prepare the way for me.". . . Jesus stops. . . . "Listen," he tells you. . . . "Listen to what John says as he baptizes each person.". . . John's voice reaches your ears. . . . "Repent and be saved," he is telling each person as he pours water over their heads.

Notice that many people are hugging each other and smiling as they leave the river. . . . Before you can ask Jesus why, he looks at you and smiles. . . . "In their hearts they want to belong to the Kingdom of my Father. . . . They now have that hope," Jesus tells you. . . .

You and Jesus enter into the river. . . . Feel the cool water splash against your legs as you slowly wade toward John. . . . As you approach John he looks deep into your eyes. . . . His strong hand touches your shoulder. . . . "Repent and be saved," he tells you as he pours water over your head. . . . Feel the cool water tickle over your face and run down onto your neck. . . .

Jesus now stands before John. . . . Do not leave. . . . Wait for Jesus. . . . Notice that John hesitates before he baptizes Jesus. . . . "I need to be baptized by you," he whispers to Jesus, . . . "and you come to me?" he asks. . . . Jesus looks into John's eyes and says, "Please do it; for I must do all that is right.". . .Jesus bows his head and John slowly pours water over the Lord's head. . . . They look at each other silently for a minute. . . . Jesus turns away, . . . takes your hand and the two of you slowly wade to shore. . . .

"Do you know what has just happened to you?" Jesus asks. . . . He does not wait for you to respond, . . . but leads you down a path along the river. . . . He stops, . . . looks at you and places his hands on your shoulders. . . . "You have just joined with those who are seeking the Kingdom of my Father. . . . You now belong to a special people.". . . The Lord smiles, . . . takes your hands in his and says, "I will show you the way to my Father's Kingdom. . . . Will you follow me?"

I will give you a time of silence to be with Jesus.

Prayer

Jesus, I'm glad that I belong to your Father's house. Teach me and help me to live my life as a member of the family of your Father. It is good to have you as my brother. Yes, Lord, I will follow you. (Invite spontaneous prayer.)

Journal Writing

Write your experience and thoughts in your journal. Write down your feeling about belonging to God's Kingdom and having Jesus as your brother. Ask Jesus to help you.

Sharing

Would anyone like to share their experience and thoughts with the class? How does it feel to know that you belong to the family of God? Does this make you special? Why? In families everyone has a responsibility. What are some of these responsibilities? What do you think are some of the responsibilities that go with belonging to the family of God? Can you think of times in your life when it may become hard to follow God's family rules?

Follow-up

(Before class prepare 6" × 8" cards for each child in the class. Score the cards in half lengthwise so that they will be easy to fold.) On the board write the following suggested slogans: "first name belongs to Jesus;" "Jesus is my brother;" "God is my Father;" "I am the son/daughter of the King."

Tell the children that they are going to make "Reminder Cards," to help them when they feel alone or are hurting in some way. They can choose one of the slogans from the board or make up their own slogan. Have them decorate the cards and fold where they are scored. They are to take their "Reminder Cards" home and place them where they can see them each day.

Closing Prayer

Gather the children in a circle around the Bible and Candle. Join hands and say together the "Our Father." (Invite spontaneous prayer if you wish.) Close with a song.

Music

"There's a New Life in Jesus," from *Cry Hosanna* (Hope Publications); "We Have Been Baptized in Christ" from *Young People's Glory and Praise* (NALR).

"City of God" from *Lord of Light* (NALR).

"Isaiah 49" from *I Will Not Forget You* (NALR).

Jesus and the Woman at the Well

John 4:1–33

Introduction

There are many people in this world who are not accepted by others. Can you name groups of people who are not accepted? Why are they not accepted? In Jesus' time there was a group of people whom the Jews did not accept. They were called Samaritans. Hundreds of years before, they had intermarried with non-Jews. This practice was forbidden by Jewish law; so the Jews did not tolerate the Samaritans. In fact, to call someone a Samaritan would be considered an insult.

We are going to be with Jesus and find out why he ignored the law and talked to a Samaritan woman.

Meditation

Close your eyes. . . . Take a deep breath, . . . and relax . . . . You are resting with Jesus beside a well in Samaria. . . . Both of you are hot and tired. . . . The journey you are making from Judea to Galilee is long. . .and you have been walking for almost two days. . . . The disciples have gone into town to buy food, leaving you alone with Jesus. . . .

It is noon and the sun is hot. . . . You and Jesus are thirsty but there is no way you can draw water from the well for you do not have a bucket or a water jar with you. . . . A Samaritan woman approaches. . . . She has a water jar with her. . . . It is a helpless feeling to know that because the Jewish law forbids you to talk to her. . . you have to remain thirsty. . . . Experience your frustration. . . .

Jesus looks at the woman. . . . She pretends she doesn't see him and busies herself letting down her jar into the well. . . . Suddenly Jesus turns to her and asks, "Will you give us a drink?" . . . The woman ignores Jesus' request. . . . Jesus watches her in silence. . . . She turns to him with questioning eyes. . . . "You are a Jew and I am a Samaritan woman," she responds brusquely. . . . Jesus nods and continues to look at her. . . . "Anyway, your law forbids that you speak to me." . . . Jesus sighs but does not respond. . . . She turns to leave and your heart sinks. . . . For a minute you could almost taste the refreshing water. . . . The woman stops . . . and turns to face Jesus. . . . Her voice is filled with sarcasm, "Here, take your water," she says and hands the water jar to him. . . . "After all it is your law you are breaking, not mine," . . . Jesus and you gulp down the water in gratitude. . . . As he hands the water jar back to her Jesus asks her why she comes at noon to draw water, when other women come in the morning or evening. . . . Quickly taking back her water jar from Jesus the woman responds. . . . "I just prefer to draw my water now!" . . . Jesus looks directly into her eyes and asks, . . . "Why is that?" . . . The woman becomes uncomfortable and shifts from foot to foot. . . . Avoiding the Lord's eyes, she responds in almost a whisper, . . . "I'm not very well accepted in town." . . . "Come," Jesus tells her, "sit down and tell me about yourself. . . . The Lord's act of kindness brings tears to the woman's eyes. . . .

She sits down next to Jesus and begins to talk about her problems. . . . Her story is sad. . . . She is not accepted by her own people because of the way she lives. . . . She has had many husbands. In fact, the one she lives with now is not really her husband. . . . She has tried to make friends but people just laugh at her and turn their backs. . . . She would like to run away, . . . but where would she go? . . . How would she live? . . .

Jesus listens and encourages her to tell him everything. . . . His kindness is too much for her and she begins to sob uncontrollably. . . . The Lord places his hand on hers. . . . "What can I do?" she pleads between sobs. . . . Looking at Jesus with a faint flicker of hope in her eyes she asks, . . . "Will you help me?". . .

Jesus nods and begins to tell her about "the living water" that will be like a spring within her welling up to eternal life. . . . The woman becomes calm and her face relaxes into a peaceful expression. . . . She no longer has to defend herself. . . . She is being accepted and understood. . . . As Jesus continues to speak to her she becomes more and more excited. . . . Suddenly she gets up. . . . "I have to go and tell the people in town about you and what you told me," she exclaims as she begins to rush off. . . . "Stay here, don't leave," she calls back as she rushes up the path to town. . . .

Jesus turns to you. . . . There is a look of sadness in his eyes. . . . "Tell me, he asks you, "who has the right to judge others. . . . to tell them or to let them know by their actions that they are not worthwhile?" Without waiting for you to reply, Jesus continues. . . . Pointing to the path the woman had taken he says, "Do you see how not accepting others kills their spirit? . . . their hope in life? . . . Is this the kind of treatment that helps people become what my Father intends them to be? . . . Jesus watches your face and waits for your response. . . .

I will give you time to answer Jesus. . . . Listen to him. . . . He will teach you what he wants you to learn about accepting others. . . .

Prayer

Jesus, forgive me, for there are people in my life that I find hard to accept. Help me to see what I do to them when I ignore them. Lord, I know that you love me and want me to help you bring hope to others and to let them know that they are worthwhile. When I am tempted to turn away from someone, I will go to you, for I know you will help me. (Invite spontaneous prayer.)

It is time to leave. . . . Say good-bye to Jesus. . . . Get up and begin to walk away. . . . Turn and wave. . . . Open your eyes, . . . and come back into the room.

Journal Writing

Write your thoughts and feelings in your journals. Ask Jesus to help you.

Sharing

How do you suppose other people your age feel when they are not accepted? How do people show that they do not accept someone? What are some of the ways people show others that they do accept them? (List these on the board.)

Follow-up

Pass out construction paper to the class. Ask the children to trace their hand and wrist on the paper and cut it out. On the wrist write THE JESUS HAND. On each finger have the class write a way to reach out to someone. At the end of class they will take the "Jesus Hands" home and place them by their bed as a reminder of how they can reach out to others this week. Next week they will bring their hands back and share their experiences with the class. They will be given an opportunity to write these experiences in their journals.

Closing Prayer

Gather around the Bible and candle. Invite each one to place their "Jesus Hand" on the Bible and ask God's blessing on what they are about to do this week.

Close by joining hands and singing.

Music

"Let There Be Peace on Earth" from *Young People's Glory and Praise* (NALR).

"Come to the Water" from *Wood Hath Hope* (NALR).

Following Jesus

Luke 6:12–42; Matthew 12:15–21; Mark 3:13–19

Introduction

Imagine that you were chosen to be on the school basketball team, or the school band. How would you feel? Now imagine that you found out how much free time you had to give up. Would you have second thoughts? Has anyone here ever been chosen for a special activity and realized later what you had to give up? What were some of the things you had to sacrifice? I wonder if the twelve apostles felt the same way you did after they were chosen by Jesus. Remember, they were human just like you and me. Let's visit Jesus and the apostles. Jesus has just chosen them to be on his special team—the Jesus Team.

Meditation

Close your eyes. . . . Take a deep breath . . . and relax. . . . Jesus and his apostles have just come down from a mountain where the Lord had chosen them to be his special followers. . . . They must have felt very privileged, don't you think? . . . However, they do not have time to think about it, because they are greeted by a large crowd. . . . Many people are waiting for Jesus to heal them. . . . Others are eagerly looking forward to his teachings. . . . It is only after Jesus has made his way to a small hill with the help of his newly chosen apostles . . . and begins to speak, . . . that the crowd becomes quiet. . . .

You are seated with the twelve apostles at the feet of Jesus. . . . Peter who sits next to you is out of breath. . . . He turns to you and says, . . . "That was hard work getting this crowd settled down." . . . John, who is sitting next to Peter is wiping his face. . . . He looks at Peter, . . . smiles at you . . . and says, "You can say that again." . . . Jesus now begins to speak. . . .

He is telling the people to love those who do not like them, . . . to do good to those who insult them. . . . And when people hurt them, Jesus says not to hurt them in return. . . . Peter touches your arm to get your attention. . . . "Do you think you could do good to someone who doesn't like you?" . . . It is a difficult question. . . . You will need time to think about it. . . . Peter watches your face for a moment, . . . smiles, . . . and turns toward Jesus. . . .

"Do not judge or condemn others or you will be judged and condemned," Jesus continues. . . . "And when you lend money, do not hope to get it back. . . . "Treat others as you would like them to treat you. . . . Give, and it will be given to you. A good measure, pressed down, shaken together and running over, will be poured into your lap. For with the measure you use, it will be measured to you. . . . If you do these things your reward will be great in heaven." . . .

Jesus finishes his teaching and everyone crowds around him . . . asking questions all at once. . . . Peter and John get up to leave. . . . "Come on," Peter tells you. . . . Some of the other apostles also leave. . . . You walk with them toward a few trees at the edge of the field . . . and sit in their shade. . . . No one is talking. . . . Their faces are serious. . . . Some are frowning.

Study Peter. . . . He's wondering if he will be able to keep out of a fight if someone starts it? . . . He's a tough fisherman who is used to having his own way. . . . What about Matthew? . . . Right now he must be in deep thought for his eyes are lowered and he is frowning. . . . Having been a tax collector all his life, . . . collecting money from people, . . . and even cheating people by charging too much interest. . . . Will he be able to lend money and not expect to get it returned to him? . . . He would have to change drastically. . . . Look at James and John. . . . They are called the "sons of thunder," because they have a bad temper. . . . Will they be able to hold off judging others when they are angry? . . . Now that these chosen men know what Jesus expects of them, . . . will they continue to follow him, . . . or, will they quit? . . .

The crowd is gone. . . . Jesus walks over to where you and the apostles are sitting. . . . "Why all the long faces?" he asks. . . . Peter looks at Jesus. . . . He seems worried. . . . "Lord, what you just taught seems impossible for me to do." . . . Jesus walks over to him, . . . stoops down, . . . and places his hand on Peter's shoulder. . . . "Don't worry Peter, I'll help you when it seems like you can't do it.". . .

Jesus straightens up and turns toward you. . . . "Do you believe that we are friends?" he asks. . . . "Does a friend help another friend when in need?". . . You silently nod. . . . Jesus continues to look at you. . . . "Then, do you believe that I, your friend, will help you when you come to me?". . . Jesus walks over to you and places his arm around your shoulders. . . . "Will you promise to come to me when you need help to be generous, . . . kind, . . . and forgiving?" he asks you.

I will give you a quiet time to respond to Jesus.

Prayer

Jesus, I believe that you are my friend. When I find it hard to do what you want me to do I will come to you for help. (Invite spontaneous prayer.) It is time to leave. . . . Say good-bye to Jesus . . . and to the apostles. . . . Turn and leave them. . . . Open your eyes . . . and come back into the room.

Journal Writing

Write down your thoughts and feelings while you were with Jesus and his apostles. Ask Jesus to help you.

Sharing

Would anyone share their experience with the class? How do you feel when someone is unkind to you,. . .or judges you wrongly? . . . How do you feel when someone doesn't forgive you? Do you see this happening among those you know? Do adults do this to each other? We can change the world around us. . .in our family, neighborhood and school. Jesus taught us to be generous, kind and forgiving. (List these in three columns on the board.) Let's suggest ways we can practice these teachings of Jesus in our own world.

Follow-up

Before class cut out two 12" diameter circles: one painted black on posterboard and one painted bright yellow on paper. Cut the yellow circle in small pie-shaped pieces.

Show the class the black circle. Tell them that it represents the world around them. They are going to bring light into the world by practicing some of the suggestions on the board. Ask the children to keep tract of the number of times they practice what Jesus taught. Next week they will count the number of times they reached out to someone in love and will paste that number of yellow pieces on top of the black circle. They will see for themselves how they help bring the light of Jesus into the world.

(The children might need more pieces of yellow. Next week prepare thin strips of bright orange paper to paste on top of the yellow if needed.)

Closing Prayer

Sit in a semi-circle around the Bible and candle. Place the black circle on the floor in the center of the circle. Give each child one or two pieces of the yellow paper.

Teacher: Jesus, we need your help to bring happiness to others. Help us to bring your light into the world around us. (Invite spontaneous prayer.) Ask the children to place their yellow pieces around the world but not on it. Tell them that the world is waiting for them.

Close with a song.

Music

"Be Not Afraid," "Like a Sunflower," and "Look Beyond," from *Young People's Glory and Praise* (NALR).

Jesus Feeds the Crowd

Matthew 14:13–22; Mark 6:30–44; Luke 9:10–17

Introduction

Do you know what the initials F.H.B. mean? It means "family-hold-back." It is used when unexpected company arrives just at meal time and there is not enough food to go around. Your mother or father will quietly tell the family not to ask for second helpings, or not to take too much food. Today, we are going to be with Jesus when a few people were asked to share their food with others.

Meditation

Close your eyes. . . . Take a deep breath . . . and relax. . . . You are in a boat on the Sea of Galilee with Jesus and his disciples. . . . Jesus has found out that Herod has had John the Baptist killed. . . . The Lord is very sad and wants to be alone. . . .

As you near the shore, you and the disciples notice that there is a large crowd waiting for Jesus. . . . Peter turns to Jesus, "Look, Lord, on that grassy hill to your left. . . . There must be hundreds of people!". . . . John turns to Jesus and sighs, "I'm afraid they are waiting for you. . . . They must have walked miles around the edge of the Sea to get here.". . . . Jesus silently watches the crowd gather. . . .

The boat lands and Jesus and his disciples start walking toward the waiting crowd. . . . You help Peter pull the boat onto the beach. . . . By the time you catch up to the others, Jesus is already walking among the people, . . . blessing and healing them. . . . More and more people arrive and soon there is a great multitude surrounding Jesus. . . .

25

It is only when Peter says, "It is getting late, Lord," that you realize the day is almost over. . . . "Send the crowd away," Peter
continues, "So they can go to their villages and buy themselves
some food.". . . Jesus turns to Peter and says, "They do not need
to go away. . . . You give them something to eat.". . . Before Peter can respond Jesus has turned from him and is blessing a
child. . . . Peter shrugs his shoulders . . . and turns to the other
disciples and tells them to spread the word and see if anyone has
brought food with them.

A little later you, Jesus and the disciples are looking at the five
loaves of bread and two fish in front of you. . . . "That will never
begin to feed. . . ." Thomas begins to say, . . . but Jesus interrupts him. . . . "Invite the people to sit down on the grass.". . . As
the word passes . . . people begin to sit down. . . . Jesus blesses
the bread and fish and offers a prayer of thanksgiving. . . . He
turns to you and hands you a half loaf of bread. . . . "Pass this
out to the people," he tells you. . . . Take the bread from Jesus
and begin to walk among the crowd. . . . Break off chunks of the
bread and give it to them. . . . Notice that their faces are smiling
and that each person thanks you as he holds up his hand to receive the bread. . . . Andrew is following you with a piece of fish,
. . . breaking some off and giving it to the people. . . . Soon your
bread is gone. . . . Return to Jesus and sit next to him. . . . Slowly
the other disciples join you. . . . Jesus breaks off pieces of his
bread and fish and shares it with you. . . . Share yours with Peter
who is sitting next to you. . . . Watch as Peter shares his bread
and fish with John. . . . In a few minutes all of you are eating
your fill.

Jesus turns to you. . . . "I see some people with baskets," he
says. "Ask them for the use of their baskets so that we can collect
the left-over food.". . . You and the disciples collect the left-over
food. . . . When you return to Jesus you have twelve baskets
filled with left-over food. . . . Seeing the surprised look on your
face, Jesus invites you to sit down next to him. . . .

"Sharing with others is my Father's wish," Jesus begins. . . .
"Isn't it often true that people will not share because they are
afraid they will not have enough for themselves?". . . Jesus
looks at the 5,000 people before him. . . . For a few minutes he is

silent. . . . He turns to you and continues to speak. . . . "When one shares God's gifts there is always enough to go around. . . . Are you willing to live your life acting on this truth?". . . Jesus looks into your eyes and waits for your response.

I will leave you alone with Jesus so that you can talk this over with him.

Prayer

Jesus, give me a generous heart. Help me to share with others, even when it is hard. Thank you for teaching me this lesson. (Invite spontaneous prayer.)

It is time to leave. . . . Say good-bye to Jesus. . . . Open your eyes and come back into the room.

Journal

Write your thoughts, feelings and experiences in your journal. Ask Jesus to help you.

Sharing

Would anyone like to share his experience with the class? Why is it important to share food with others? Do you think the 5,000 people were grateful for the food? Does anyone know of a place where food is given out to the poor? Besides food what other things in your life are you able to share? (List them on the board.)

Follow-up

(Before class prepare the following material: 6" diameter circles, squares or rectangles cut out of posterboard; strips of posterboard to be used as hands on the clock; punch a hole in one end large enough to hold a brad; enough brads for each person; magic markers.)

Teacher: One of the hardest things to share with others is our time. Why is it hard? Isn't it true that when you are called away from a game you are playing that you often grumble? Today you are going to make a Time-Sharing Clock. Each time you voluntarily share your time with someone you will move the minute hand ahead one number. When the minute hand has gone all around the clock you will move the hour hand ahead one number. The one rule is: you must share your time pleasantly, if you grumble you cannot move the minute hand ahead a number.

As you begin to make your Time-Sharing Clock study the list on the board for ideas on how to share time.

Closing Prayer

Gather around the Bible and candle. Invite the class to plan a way they might share their time with someone. Invite spontaneous prayer asking Jesus to help them. Close with a song.

Music

"Look Beyond" from *Young People's Glory and Praise* (NALR).

"Bread Blessed and Broken" from *Star-light* (NALR).

"We are Your Bread" by Joe Wise (World Library Publications).

Your Place in the Kingdom

Mark 10:35–45; Luke 22:24–27; Matthew 20:20–28

Introduction

Many names of important people are mentioned in newspapers and on television. Can anyone give me some of these names and tell me why these people are special or important? (List them on the board.) How would you like to have your name mentioned on television or in the newspapers? How would you feel? Do you want to feel special or important?

James and his brother John wanted to be important and so they decided to do something about it. We are going to be with them and see what Jesus has to say about being important.

Meditation

Close your eyes. . . . Take a deep breath . . . and relax. . . . You are walking with Jesus along a hot dusty road. . . . The disciples are walking behind you in groups of two and three. . . . It is too hot to hurry . . . or even to do much talking. . . . Jesus calls your attention to a bird nesting in a tree. . . . It looks like it is panting from the heat; its mouth is open. . . .

Someone from behind calls out, . . . " Jesus, wait for us.". . . You turn to see James and John hurrying up to you. . . . Jesus stops and waits for them. . . . "We have a favor to ask of you," John says. . . . "What is this favor you want of me?" Jesus asks them. . . . John quickly glances at his brother . . . and then begins to speak, "We were wondering. . .when you become ruler of your Kingdom can we sit beside you, and.". . . James interrupts John and continues, "Could we be your special ministers of state?"... They wait silently for Jesus to answer their request.... Jesus rubs his beard and studies them....

"Sooo, ... you want to be my special ministers of state do you?" the Lord questions.... "Oh, yes, Lord," the brothers enthusiastically respond.... Jesus studies them for a moment.... "Are you willing to share the hardships that go with the job?" Jesus asks.... "Yes, Lord," John answers.... His eyes are dancing with excitement....

The other apostles join you.... "What's going on?" Peter asks you.... As you tell him what has been happening he becomes angry.... His eyes dart furiously toward James and John.... "Just who do they think they are?" Peter questions angrily.... Jesus turns toward Peter and sees his anger. "Come," let's rest a while," Jesus tells everyone. "I have something to say to you."... Everyone sits down close to Jesus, except James and John.... They sit a little apart from the others and avoid looking at them.... Their faces are red with embarrassment....

"Now," Jesus begins, "you know that those who rule the country show their importance or authority by commanding others to serve them.... But I do not want you to do this.... My Kingdom is ruled differently."... Andrew looks puzzled.... "What is different in your Kingdom, Lord?" he asks.... Jesus looks at Andrew and explains that in his Kingdom, anyone who wants to become great must serve others.... The apostles begin to mumble to each other.... Jesus waits for them to become silent.... "Haven't you been helping me minister to others, ... not only healing the sick but teaching them about the Kingdom?" The apostles nod.... Jesus smiles at them.... "I have chosen you to be my friends and to help me to do my Father's will on earth."... Jesus does not wait for anyone to reply to what he just said, but continues, ... "You are special to me because you are who you are.... Do not concern yourselves about becoming important by seeking jobs that the world says are important."... Jesus stands and there is a smile on his face and a look of love in his eyes as he studies his followers.... "You are already special.... You are already important because you are mine and my Father has called you to His Kingdom."... The tension at the beginning has disappeared and the apostles begin to smile and talk to each other. . . .

Jesus turns to you, . . .reaches out and places his arm around your shoulder. . .and smiles. . . . "So, my friend, why is it so hard for you to believe that you are very special to me? . . .

I will give you a quiet time to talk to Jesus about this.

Prayer

Jesus, I want to be special. Help me to believe that I am. There are times in my life when I feel unimportant. I need your help during these times. Thank you for showing me that I am special. (Invite spontaneous prayer.)

It is time to leave. Say good-bye to Jesus and begin to walk away. Open your eyes and come back into the room.

Journal Writing

Write down the thoughts and feelings you had while you were with Jesus and his apostles. Ask Jesus to help you understand how you are special.

Sharing

Does anyone wish to share their experience with the class? There are many ways in which we differ from each other. Who can name some of the ways? (List them on the board.) Can you see that no two people are alike? Not only are we different from each other, but each person is special. Jesus told you the reason why you are special and most important to God. In what ways are we special? (List them on the board.)

Follow-up

We need to remind ourselves that we are special. Therefore, we are going to make a "Reminder Card" for ourselves.

(Pass out an 8 × 3 inch piece of posterboard to each person. Punch holes at either end of the top. Cut different colored yarn long enough to hang the cards. Write the following on the board:

_____ IS SPECIAL TO GOD

(The child's first name is printed here.)

Ask the class to decorate the cards and knot yarn into the two holes. Tell them that they are to take them home and hang them where they can see them.)

Closing Prayer

Sit in a circle around the Bible and candle. Each person places his "Reminder Card" in front of him. Invite the class to pass their cards around the circle so that others can see it. Call attention to the different designs on the card.

The teacher begins prayer by thanking God for being special to Him.

Invite others to thank God for making them special.

Close with a song of praise.

Music

"Great Things Happen" from *Young People's Glory and Praise* (NALR).

"You Are My Friends" from *You Are My Friends* (NALR).

"Beatitudes" from *Beginning Today* (NALR).

Who Is My Neighbor?

Luke 10:29–37

Introduction

Who is your neighbor? Are you friendly with your neighbor? Do you live in a neighborhood where people not only talk to each other but help each other? Can you give an example of this? Jesus teaches that a neighbor is someone who is friendly and caring. According to Jesus, a person doesn't have to live next door to you to be your neighbor. We are going to be with Jesus and listen to what he teaches about being a neighbor.

Meditation

Close your eyes. . . . Take a deep breath . . . and relax. . . . You are with Jesus and his disciples traveling toward Jerusalem. . . . It has been a long journey . . . and the sun's rays beat down on you making the journey unpleasant. . . . Peter takes his handkerchief and wipes the perspiration off his face. . . . He sees that you are hot and tired and smiles sympathetically. . . . "We are almost to the next town," he tells you. . . . "You'll have a chance to rest and cool off.". . .

John, who is walking ahead with Jesus, turns around and calls to you, . . . "The town is just ahead. . . . I see it.". . . As you approach the town, the first thing you see is a crowd of people who are coming down the road to meet Jesus. . . . Jesus stops and waits for you to catch up to him. . . . "Let's walk over to those shade trees just ahead," Jesus says. . . . "We need to get out of this hot sun."

People begin to arrive where you are resting and sit down near Jesus. . . . A woman comes forward and offers Jesus a drink from her water jar. . . . Jesus smiles gratefully, . . . thanks

her, . . . takes a drink, and passes the water jar to his disciples. . . .

The townspeople are soon gathered around Jesus and silently
wait for him to speak. . . . A middle-aged man asks Jesus what
he must do to receive eternal life. . . . "He's a teacher of the
Law," John whispers to you. . . . Jesus answers him, "Love the
Lord your God with all your heart, . . . soul, . . . strength, and
mind, . . . and love your neighbor as yourself." The teacher nods,
and then asks, "Who is my neighbor?". . . A child raises his hand
excitedly. . . . "I know who *my* neighbor is!" he exclaims as he
points to an old man sitting near him. . . . "He's my neighbor because he lives next door to me!". . . . The child sits down with a
smile of satisfaction on his face. . . . People nod and smile at the
happy child. . . . Jesus also smiles. . . .

"I will tell you a story," he says. . . . By the expressions of interest on the faces of the crowd you can see that they like to be told
stories. . . . "There was once a man who was going from Jerusalem to Jericho," Jesus begins. . . . "Robbers attacked him, beat
him and left him half dead.". . . A look of concern is written on
the faces of the children. . . . Jesus continues his story, telling
about a priest and then a Levite who saw the victim but passed
him by. . . . "But a Samaritan who was traveling that way came
upon the man and was filled with pity. . . . He went over to him
and began to take care of his wounds. . . . He then put the man
on his animal and took him to an inn. . . . 'Take care of him,' he
told the innkeeper, 'and when I come back this way I will pay
you for whatever you spend.' "

Jesus looks at the teacher of the law and asks, "In your opin-
ion, which one of these three acted like a neighbor toward the
man attacked by robbers?". . . Someone in the crowd speaks
out, "Why, the one who was kind to him, of course.". . . The
teacher of the Law answers, "The one who was kind to
him.". . . . Jesus nods his head and says, "You go, then, and do
the same."

Jesus turns to you. . .and places his hand on your shoulder. . . . The touch of Jesus' hand on your shoulder makes you
feel very special, doesn't it? . . . Jesus smiles. . . . His face now
becomes serious. . . . "What I ask of all my friends is to be a car-

ing person, . . . to reach out and help others when they are in need. . . . Will you do this?". . . Jesus keeps looking into your eyes and waits for you to answer him. . . .

I will give you a silent time so that you can talk to Jesus. . . .

Prayer

Jesus, I will try to be a caring person. Teach me to help others and show them I care. (Invite spontaneous prayer.)

It is time to leave Jesus. . . . Say good-bye. . . . Open your eyes . . . and come back into the room.

Journal Writing

Write down your experience, thoughts and feelings while you were with Jesus. Write down your answer to Jesus' question. He will help you. Ask him.

Sharing

Would anyone care to share their thoughts about caring for others? What would have happened to the man attacked by the robbers if no one stopped to help him? According to Jesus' teaching, who is a neighbor? Why is it important to show others you care? Have you ever experienced being hurt and finding out that no one cared? How did you feel? The Samaritan not only felt sorry for the man, but he went out of his way to take care of him. Therefore, what is Jesus telling you to do? There are many opportunities throughout your week where you can reach out to someone and show them that you care. Can you think of possible opportunities?

Follow-up

(Prepare before class: pieces of heavy posterboard approximately 1½ inch square with holes punched out at the top, short pieces of yarn; small safety pins; felt markers and crayons)

Tell the class that this week they are to try to be aware of others and reach out to let them know they care. The opportunities are all around them, in school, at home, in their neighborhood, everywhere. They will begin to see this as they practice being aware of others. To remind themselves and others that they care, they will make "I Care" buttons. Make the letters large and dark so others can see them. They can color and design their buttons if they wish. When they come to class next week they will share their experience.

Closing Prayer

Have the children bring their "I Care" buttons to the semi-circle and sit around the Bible and candle. Tell them to place their buttons around the Bible.

Teacher: "Jesus, help us to go out this week and show others we care. Give us the courage to reach out to others and bring your Light into their lives. Bless us, Lord as we try to follow your teaching." As the children sing an appropriate song, have the class walk over to the Bible, pick up their buttons, and pin them on.

Music

"Reach Out" and "Service" from *Young People's Glory and Praise* (NALR).

"Whatsoever You Do" by Willard F. Tabusch (ACTA Foundation).

Like Lilies of the Field

Matthew 6:25–34; Luke 12:22–31

Introduction

What are some of the things you worry about? (Head three columns on the board: "Worry" - "The Reason" - "What can be done about it?" As the children share a worry write it on the board. Have them give a reason for the worry, and write it down. The last column is left until after the meditation.) Let's go to Jesus and listen to what he tells us about worry.

Meditation

Close your eyes. . . . Take a deep breath . . . and relax. . . . You are in a large field. . . . The sky is blue and cloudless. . . . Feel the warm sun on your head. . . . Start walking through the field. . . . The weeds brush against your legs as you walk. . . . They tickle, don't they? . . . Notice all the flowers. . . . They are everywhere, . . . especially the pink and white lilies. . . . Butterflies flutter from one flower to the next. . . . See the different species of butterflies. . . . You can tell by their coloring. . . .

Listen to the birds singing and calling out to each other. . . . They are resting on branches of the trees just ahead. . . . Walk over to the trees. . . . A group of men are sitting in their cool shade. . . . As you walk closer you recognize that the men are Jesus and his disciples. . . .

They see you and call out your name and invite you to join them. . . . Jesus smiles up at you, . . . pats the ground next to him and invites you to sit down beside him. . . . It feels good to be wanted, doesn't it? . . . especially by Jesus and his friends. . . .

Judas had been talking to Jesus before you arrived . . . and now he continues. . . . He is telling Jesus that he is worried about the little money they have to buy food. . . . The Lord turns to him, "Judas, why are you always so worried about money?" he asks. Turning to you and the others he says, "Do not worry about your life, what you will eat . . . or drink . . . or wear. . . ."

A bird perched on a branch just above you begins to sing. . . . Jesus places his arm around your shoulders . . . and points to the bird. . . . "Look at that little fellow," Jesus laughs. . . . "It neither plants, harvests, or stores its food for the future, . . . yet your heavenly Father feeds him.". . . Jesus gives you a little hug and asks, . . . "Are you not much more valuable than that little bird?"

Before you can answer Jesus points to the lilies in the field. . . . "See how the lilies of the field grow? . . . They neither labor or spin, yet the richest person in the world could never look more beautiful, . . . no matter how much money they spend on their clothes. . . ." Jesus points to a pink lily that is beginning to wilt. . . . "That one will not last until tomorrow, . . . yet my Father cares for it.". . .

Turning to you Jesus asks, . . . "Do you understand what I am teaching you? . . . You are more valuable than all of these. . . . Will not my Father then, take care of you more than these?". . . Jesus waits, . . . looks into your eyes, . . .and finally speaks. . . . "Now tell me all that you worry about. . . . Let me help you.". . .

I will give you time now to talk and listen to Jesus. . . . Talk to him about your worries, . . . what makes you unhappy, . . . what makes you happy. . . .

Closing Prayer

Jesus, I'm glad you let me talk to you about my worries and problems. I feel better now because you listened to me. When I start worrying I'll come to you and we'll talk about it. Thank you, Jesus, for loving me and helping me. I love you. (Invite the children to pray aloud.)

It is time to leave. . . . Say good-bye to Jesus. . . . Get up and begin to walk away. . . . Turn and give one last wave. . . . Open your eyes and come back into the room.

Journal Writing

Now that you have talked and listened to Jesus, write in your journals the thoughts you have about facing your worries. Write any thoughts that might come to you even if they are not about worrying.

Sharing Time

Does anyone have any special thought about worrying that would help the rest of us? Let's go to our third column on the board and fill it in.

Follow-up

The aim of the following activity is to help the class express their thoughts verbally in a given situation and to help them see that they often create their own worries. Puppets will be used for the following role-play. The use of puppets may be less threatening for a child and will allow the shy child to express himself or herself. The conflict situation can be adjusted to meet the needs of the group.

Plot

Jim (Mary) is worried about a play-off game he is in and knows the need of a final practice before the game. However, his friend wants him to watch a double feature on cable television with him. (Let the class suggest two popular films.) Jim has two choices: to practice or to watch cable television.

I want two people to play the part of Jim (Mary) and his friend in scene one: Jim decides to watch television; and in scene two: Jim decides to practice.

Discussion: Do we often create our own worries?

Closing Prayer

(Gather in a semi-circle around the Bible and candle.)

Teacher: Let's go to Jesus under the shade trees in the field. (Allow a few seconds for the class to go to their place.)

Teacher shares a thought from her journal (similar to the following): Jesus, when I worry, I know that I do not trust you to take care of me. I know you will help me do my part.

Invite others to share a thought from their journal, or thank Jesus.

Read Matthew 6:25.

Close with a song.

Music

"Bloom Where Your're Planted" and "Only a Shadow" from *Young People's Glory and Praise* (NALR).

The Pharisee and the Tax Collector

Luke 18:9–14

Introduction

To decide something in your mind is to make a judgment. This is good, because God gave us this gift. However, people often misuse their gift by judging others. Have you ever heard someone say, "Oh, he/she is a poor sport, lazy, or a trouble-maker?" How would you feel if someone said that about you? Do they have a right to judge you? Why? Why not? Jesus has something to say about judging others. We are going to be with him and listen to his teaching about judging others.

Meditation

Close your eyes. . . . Take a deep breath . . . and relax. . . . You are with Jesus and his disciples sitting by a creek. . . . Your journey today has been long and hot. . . . All of you are tired. . . . Some of you are dangling your feet in a cool stream. . . . Feel the water splashing over your feet and ankles. . . . It feels, good, doesn't it? . . . Peter wades into the creek and sighs, "Ahhh, this feels so good.". . . John and Andrew join him. . . . You all begin to relax and enjoy yourselves. . . . Some of the disciples begin to joke and tease each other. . . .

A few people from the nearby town walk up and stare at you. . . . "Look at you!" a man scornfully remarks. . . . His nose seems pinched tight and his mouth curled down in displeasure. . . . Turning to his friends, he points to Jesus and says, "And to think we are supposed to listen to this teacher's great words of wisdom!". . . Jesus turns to them. . . . "Come join us, " he says with a smile. . . . Without responding, the men turn their backs and walk to a nearby tree and sit down. . . . You can tell that they mean to continue their observations so that they can tell others. . . .

"Well, that's that," Peter sighs and wades out of the creek. . . . The fun and relaxation have suddenly disappeared. . . . One by one the other disciples leave the creek and put on their sandals. . . . "It is time to leave anyway," Jesus remarks as he puts on his sandals. . . . "There are people gathering.". . . As you walk over to the large crowd now gathering, you notice that your "critics" have joined the crowd. . . .

Jesus begins his teaching by telling a story. . . . "Once there were two men who went up to the Temple to pray; one was a Pharisee, the other a tax collector. The Pharisee stood apart by himself and prayed, 'I thank you God, that I am not greedy, dishonest, or an adulterer, like everybody else. I thank you that I am not like the tax collector over there. I fast two days a week, and I give you one tenth of all my income.". . . Jesus pauses. . . . His eyes search the crowd and focus on a Pharisee. . .whose eyes are angerly focusing on the Lord. . . . Jesus continues, . . . "But the tax collector stood at a distance and would not even raise his face to heaven, but beat on his breast and said, "God have pity on me, a sinner.". . . The crowd is very still. . . . They seem purposely to avoid glancing toward the Pharisees. . . .

"I tell you," Jesus continues, "the tax collector, and not the Pharisee, was in the right with God when he went home. . . . For everyone who makes himself great will be humbled, and everyone who humbles himself will be made great.". . . The Pharisees abruptly leave. . .and your "friendly critics" are nowhere in sight. . . .

After the last of the crowd has left, you, Jesus and the disciples gather together. . . . "Our critics didn't stay too long," Andrew remarks. . . . Jesus nods, . . . he seems sad. . . . "Who can claim to know the heart of another person?" Jesus asks. . . . "You said yourself, Lord," Andrew remarks, "that out of the mouth the heart speaks.". . . Jesus looks at him. . . . "Does that give anyone the right to judge others?". . .

Jesus places his arm around your shoulders as he continues to respond to Andrew's remark. . . . "Be merciful as your heavenly Father is merciful. . . . Do not judge lest you *yourselves* be judged.". . . "Andrew," Jesus asks, "rather than judging others, wouldn't it be better to look for the good?". . . Jesus turns to you and asks, "Will you try to do this?". . .

I will leave you alone with Jesus and his disciples. Continue to listen to what Jesus is teaching you. Ask him to help you.

Prayer

Jesus, forgive me for being critical of others. Help me to treat others as I want to be treated, not judging, but accepting them. (Invite spontaneous prayer.)

It is time to leave Jesus and his disciples. . . . Say good-bye. . . . Open your eyes. . .and come back into the room. . . .

Journal Writing

Write your experience, feelings and thoughts in your journals. Ask Jesus to help you.

Sharing

Would anyone care to share with the class the thoughts they had about judging others? Were the critics who sat under the tree misjudging Jesus, you and the disciples? What made them misjudge you? What is the difference between correcting someone and criticizing him? How do you feel when you are judged wrongly? Why? When this happens do you feel that you are not understood? Why? What does this teach you about judging others?

Follow-up

(Before class prepare a half-sheet of paper for each child with his or her name printed on it.) Tell the class that everyone likes to have their good points noticed. This does not happen very often. Therefore, today they are going to encourage each other. (Pass out the pieces of paper, make sure that no one gets his own name.) Tell the class that each one has a name of someone in the class. They are to ask Jesus to help them write down a good quality that they notice in that person. When they have finished, collect the papers.

Closing Prayer

Sit around the Bible and candle. Place the papers by the Bible. The teacher prays: "Jesus, teach us to encourage each other by acknowledging the good qualities we see. Help us not to judge others and criticize them. Thank you, Jesus, for helping us. (Give the papers to the individuals whose names are on them. Tell the class to silently read their paper and to thank God for this gift. Close with a song.

Music

"You Are Near" from *Young People's Glory and Praise* (NALR).

"Praise the Lord, My Soul" from *Earthen Vessels* (NALR).

"I tell you," Jesus continues, "the tax collector, and not the Pharisee, was in the right with God when he went home. . . . For everyone who makes himself great will be humbled, and everyone who humbles himself will be made great.". . . The Pharisees abruptly leave. . .and your "friendly critics" are no-where in sight. . . .

After the last of the crowd has left, you, Jesus and the disciples gather together. . . . "Our critics didn't stay too long," Andrew remarks. . . . Jesus nods, . . . he seems sad. . . . "Who can claim to know the heart of another person?" Jesus asks. . . . "You said yourself, Lord," Andrew remarks, "that out of the mouth the heart speaks.". . . Jesus looks at him. . . . "Does that give any-one the right to judge others?". . .

Jesus places his arm around your shoulders as he continues to respond to Andrew's remark. . . . "Be merciful as your heavenly Father is merciful.`. . . Do not judge lest you *yourselves* be judged.". . . "Andrew," Jesus asks, "rather than judging others, wouldn't it be better to look for the good?". . . Jesus turns to you and asks, "Will you try to do this?". . .

I will leave you alone with Jesus and his disciples. Continue to listen to what Jesus is teaching you. Ask him to help you.

Prayer

Jesus, forgive me for being critical of others. Help me to treat others as I want to be treated, not judging, but accepting them. (Invite spontaneous prayer.)

It is time to leave Jesus and his disciples. . . . Say good-bye. . . . Open your eyes. . .and come back into the room. . . .

Journal Writing

Write your experience, feelings and thoughts in your journals. Ask Jesus to help you.

Sharing

Would anyone care to share with the class the thoughts they had about judging others? Were the critics who sat under the tree misjudging Jesus, you and the disciples? What made them misjudge you? What is the difference between correcting someone and criticizing him? How do you feel when you are judged wrongly? Why? When this happens do you feel that you are not understood? Why? What does this teach you about judging others?

Follow-up

(Before class prepare a half-sheet of paper for each child with his or her name printed on it.) Tell the class that everyone likes to have their good points noticed. This does not happen very often. Therefore, today they are going to encourage each other. (Pass out the pieces of paper, make sure that no one gets his own name.) Tell the class that each one has a name of someone in the class. They are to ask Jesus to help them write down a good quality that they notice in that person. When they have finished, collect the papers.

Closing Prayer

Sit around the Bible and candle. Place the papers by the Bible. The teacher prays: "Jesus, teach us to encourage each other by acknowledging the good qualities we see. Help us not to judge others and criticize them. Thank you, Jesus, for helping us. (Give the papers to the individuals whose names are on them. Tell the class to silently read their paper and to thank God for this gift. Close with a song.

Music

"You Are Near" from *Young People's Glory and Praise* (NALR).

"Praise the Lord, My Soul" from *Earthen Vessels* (NALR).

Blind Bartimaeus Believes

Mark 10:46–52; Luke 18:35–43; Matthew 20:29–34

Introduction

We often find ourselves doing things we have to do, but really don't want to do; for example, homework. Do you always want to do your homework? What are the excuses students use when they do not have their homework done on time? (List them on the board.) Do you always pay attention in class? What are some reasons for not paying attention? (List them on board.) Do you feel it is important to learn? Why? When you are learning something new, do you become discouraged at times and want to give up? Wouldn't it be easy to forget everything and just have a good time? Can we do this? To do something we don't want to do, we have to persevere. What does *perseverance* mean? Why is it important to persevere? We are going to be with Jesus and meet a man who persevered.

Meditation

Close your eyes. . . . Take a deep breath . . . and relax. . . . You are with Jesus and his disciples just outside the famous and beautiful city of Jericho. . . . A large crowd surrounds you. . . . Many are pleading with Jesus to stay with them for just a little while longer. . . . You wish Jesus WOULD stay here a little longer. . . . Jericho is a wealthy city filled with beautiful houses and gardens. . . . Even the air is filled with a sweet smelling fragrance. . . . This comes from the many balsam groves that surround the city. . . . The oil from these trees is used to make medicine and perfume. . . . However, you see that Jesus is determined to be on his way. . . .

A blind begger who is sitting at the edge of one of the balsam groves calls out and asks what is happening. . . . "Why are there so many people here?" he asks anyone who is within hearing distance. . . . A man nearby tells him that Jesus of Nazareth is passing by. . . . The beggar reaches out his arms in the direction of the many voices he hears and calls out, "Jesus, Son of David, have mercy on me!". . . Jesus turns to a man standing next to him and asks who it is that is calling out to him. . . . "Oh, that's just Bartimaeus, the beggar," the man answers. . . . "He's always around begging for one thing or another.". . .

Someone from the crowd hurries over to Bartimaeus and angerly tries to silence him. . . . But Bartimaeus cries out all the louder, "Son of David, have mercy on me!". . . Jesus stops. . . . He looks toward Bartimaeus. . . . "Bring him to me," the Lord commands. . . . A man hurries up to Bartimaeus and tells him, "Take heart; rise, he is calling you.". . . With a sharp cry of joy, Bartimaeus throws off his cloak,. . .leaps up, . . . and hurries toward Jesus. . . .

"What do you want me to do for you?" Jesus asks him. . . . "Master, let me receive my sight," Bartimaeus pleads. . . . Jesus studies Bartimaeus' face for a moment and then says, "Go your way, your faith has made you well.". . . Watch Bartimaeus' face. . . . See his clouded eyes slowly become clear. . . . "I can see! . . . I can see!" he cries. . .as he looks upon the face of Jesus who is smiling at him. . . . As the crowd turns their attention toward Bartimaeus, . . . Jesus turns to you, . . . places his hand on your shoulder and whispers "Come.". . . He leads you away from the crowd. . . .

"I want to teach you something," Jesus tells you. . . . "Did you see how Bartimaeus was not discouraged when people tried to silence him?. . . It made him persevere all the more, didn't it?". . . You agree with Jesus, for you, too, had seen people angerly try to silence him. . . . "As Bartimaeus' faith in me helped him persevere," Jesus continues, "so too your faith in me will help you keep trying when things are hard.". . . Jesus places his hand on your shoulder,. . .looks into your eyes and asks, "Do you believe that you are my friend?". . . Jesus sees by the expression on your face that you do believe. . . . "Then, will you come to me and let me help you persevere? . . . Jesus waits for your answer. . . .

I will now give you a few moments of silence. What is it that you want to say to Jesus?

Prayer

Jesus, sometimes it is not easy to keep trying. I believe that you are my special friend and will help me persevere when I am ready to give up. (Invite spontaneous prayer.)

It is time to leave Jesus. . . . Say good-bye. . . . Open your eyes and come back into the room.

Journal Writing

Write your experiences, feelings and thoughts in your journal. Ask Jesus to help you.

Sharing

Would anyone like to share their experience or thoughts with the class? What would have happened to Bartimaeus if he listened to those who told him to be quiet? Even though you do not see Jesus as Bartimaeus did, he is still with you, even closer, for his Holy Spirit lives in you. Do you believe that Jesus can help you as he did Bartimaeus? Look at the board and see the excuses people use when they do not want to try. Are they excuses used to give up and not try? When you finally succeed at something, how do you feel? Was it worth all the trouble? There are people in this world who seem to accomplish impossible tasks. Can you name any of these people? There are people right around you who persevere. You are going to see if you can find these people.

Follow-up

(Before class duplicate half sheets of paper with the words WHO?, WHAT?, WHEN?, WHERE?, and WHY? written in a column on the left. Leave room for written responses to these questions. Make individual pads of five sheets for each person in the class.) On the board write: WHO?, WHAT?, WHEN?, WHERE?, and WHY? Tell the class that these are the questions that reporters ask when going after a news item. This week they are going to do some investigative reporting. There are people around them who persevere. They can be their friends, members of their family, neighbors, classmates, etc. What they are to do is to observe. If it is possible, they can interview the person and ask why he perseveres. They are to record the responses and observations in their Reporter's Notebook. Next week they will bring their news items to class and share with the others.

Closing prayer

Place the Reporters' Notebooks near the Bible. The class gathers in a semi-circle around the Bible and candle.

Teacher: "We are going to ask God's blessing on each other as we go out to find those who persevere. As an outward sign of blessing we will hold both arms out toward each other. (Pray using words like the following.) Jesus, bless us as we go out this week to find those who keep on trying."

The teacher passes out the Reporters' Notebooks as the children sing.

Music

"Son of David" from *Wood Hath Hope* (NALR).

"Glory and Praise" from *Young People's Glory and Praise* (NALR).

"Lay Your Hands" from *Abba! Father!* (NALR).

The Grateful Leper Gives Thanks

Luke 17:11-19

Introduction

Did you ever give something to someone and have that person take it and never thank you? How did you feel? Why? Have you ever helped someone and not had that person thank you? Did you wonder if what you did was satisfactory? Why is it important to thank people and to be thanked? We are going to be with Jesus and his disciples and see Jesus' reaction when he is not thanked.

Meditation

Close your eyes. . . . Take a deep breath . . . and relax. . . . You are with Jesus and his disciples on your way to Jerusalem and are just crossing the border between Galilee and Samaria. . . . Jesus' popularity has slowed the journey, . . . for many people stop him and want to be helped. . . . Matthew, who is walking beside you, begins to count, . . . "One, . . . two, . . . three, . . . four, five, six, seven, eight, nine, ten. . . . There are ten of them!" he exclaims. . . . You look to where he is pointing and see ten people standing at a distance. . . . They make no move to come closer. . . . Study these people and see their ragged and torn clothes . . . and worst of all the terrible running sores on their faces. . . . "Why don't they come closer?" you ask. . . . "They can't, because of the law," Matthew explains. . . . "You see, they are lepers and have to keep their distance.". . . . One of the lepers calls out, "Jesus, Master, have pity on us.". . . . Jesus stops, . . .he turns toward the lepers but does not answer at first. . . . The lepers do not move, . . . but silently watch Jesus. . . . The Lord calls out, . . . "Go show yourself to the priest.". . .

"A priest?. . . Why a priest?" you ask Matthew. . . . He does not answer you at first. . . . He is watching the lepers run toward the village. . . . "The priests are the official health officers," he responds still watching the retreating lepers. . . . "They are the ones who decide if you are healed. . . . It is the law.". . . Slowly, you, Jesus and the disciples begin to follow the lepers. . . . No one is speaking. . . . The sight of the lepers must have effected the others as it did you. . . .

Suddenly a man runs out of the village toward you. . . . He is shouting something. . . . You cannot make out what he is saying because he is too far away. . . . As he comes closer to Jesus he falls to the ground and begins to praise and thank God. . . . "I am healed! . . . Praise God!" he shouts. . . . At first you do not recognize him. . . . Slowly, you begin to realize that he is one of the ten lepers who were healed. . . . His face is now clear and healthy looking. . . .

Jesus looks down at him and questions, "Were not all ten made clean?. . . Where are the other nine?". . . The man looks up helplessly, for he does not seem to know what happened to his companions. . . . Jesus frowns. . . . Turning to you and the disciples he asks, . . . "Was no one found to return and give praise to God except this foreigner?". . .

"Why, he's a Samaritan!" Judas exclaims. . . . The man glances at Judas . . . and for a moment lowers his head. . . . But he is too filled with joy to contain himself . . . and he continues to thank and praise God. . . . Jesus looks at him lovingly. . . . "Rise," he tells him, "and go, your faith has made you well.". . . The Samaritan rises, . . . looks lovingly at Jesus, . . . turns, . . . and leaves. . . .

Andrew is frowning as he watches the man hurry off. . . . "Can you imagine that! . . . The only one who returns to give thanks is a Samaritan!" he exclaims. . . . "Ungrateful," mutters Peter, "Those nine were given a gift of new life and they didn't even take the time to say thanks.". . . "Lord, why don't you take your gift back?" Judas suggests. . . . Jesus does not respond. . . . He is looking toward the village. . . . He seems to be waiting for the nine to return. . . .

Go over and stand next to Jesus and wait with him. . . . Maybe the others will return. . . . Jesus looks at you. . . . There is a sadness in his eyes. . . . Turning to face Judas, Jesus says,. . . "There is a more important healing. . . . It is the healing of their hearts.". . . Turning to you, Jesus explains. . . . "You see, to show gratitude and give thanks is important . . . for doing so opens the heart of the person . . . to God. . . . The seed of love is planted in the fertile heart of the giver and the receiver. . . . And,". . . Jesus places his arm around your shoulders,. . .gives you a hug, . . . and smiles. . . . "You begin to appreciate how God takes care of you and shows His love for you through others.". . . "Come," he says, "Let me teach you how a grateful heart turns to God in praise and thanksgiving.". . .

I will give you time to be alone with Jesus and listen to what he wants to tell you.

Prayer

Jesus, I know I do not appreciate all that I have been given,. . . my family, a home, food, clothing, friends. . . . Help me to appreciate the gifts you surround me with. . . . (Invite spontaneous prayer.)

Journal

Today, as you write about your experience and feelings while you were with Jesus, ask Jesus to help you write down one special gift that he has given you.

Follow-up

(The class is seated in a circle.)

Teacher: Did anyone ever tell you how much they appreciate something about you—your generosity, your smile? Do you ever tell someone that they are a good ball player?. . . Or did you ever thank someone for helping you with your homework, telling them that they are a good student?. . . We all have special gifts and so often we feel that we are not appreciated. . . . Today we are going to have a circle of appreciation. . . . Each person will have a turn to be thanked by one or two persons in the circle. . .(No more than two persons). . . You will mention one thing you appreciate in the person and thank the person for sharing it with others.

Before we start, let us go to Jesus and ask him to be with us. . . . "Jesus, bless each of us as we reach out to each other and recognize the gifts you have given to him or her."

(To encourage the class the teacher begins.)

When the session is over ask the class how they felt when someone mentioned a gift they had and thanked them for sharing it. Ask them if they were surprised that they had that particular gift.

Close with a song.

Music

"Come, Let Us Praise Our God" from *Young People's Glory and Praise* (NALR).

"We Thank You, Father" from *Locusts and Wild Honey* (NALR).

"Song of Thanksgiving" from *Beginning Today* (NALR).

Jesus Comes to Zacchaeus' House

Luke 19:1–10

Introduction

When you were little did you know the dangers of crossing the street? How did you learn to look both ways before crossing? Are you wiser now about safety? Let's compare the things you know now with what you knew when you were little. For example, what happens when you don't obey your parents or teacher? Did you have to learn how important this is through possibly unpleasant experiences? There are other kinds of growth, besides physical. Name some other ways in which you've grown. There is still another way to grow and this is the most important growth in our lives. Who can name it? Why is this growth so important to us?

There was a man named Zacchaeus who met and talked to Jesus. He wanted to grow closer to God. We are going to be with Zacchaeus and Jesus when they first met.

Meditation

Close your eyes. . . . Take a deep breath . . . and relax. . . . You are entering the town of Jericho with Jesus and his disciples. It is a very beautiful place. . . . The perfume of the balsam groves fills the air. . . . Balsam trees are used for their oil which makes medicine and perfume. . . . There are beautiful flowers of all colors everywhere. . .and sycamore trees line the city streets. . . . "Smell the air," Jesus says,. . .pointing to the balsam groves in the distance. . . . "It is filled with perfume from those balsam trees.". . . Jesus stops and points to a rose bush in a flower garden. . . . He looks at you and smiles. . . . "Aren't those red roses beautiful?" he asks. . . .

A crowd begins to gather around Jesus, you and the disciples. . . . They are anxious to talk to Jesus. . .and as they press in you feel almost suffocated. . . . A man begins to call out. . . . "Let me through, I can't see him.". . . James touches your arm and calls your attention to a short, fat man jumping up and down behind the crowd. . . . The people ignore him,. . .but the man continues to jump up and down,. . .trying to see over the crowd. . . . Jesus begins to make his way through the crowd with the help of James and John. . . . The man who was jumping up and down suddenly runs up the street ahead of you and climbs a sycamore tree. . . . Judas watches the man and remarks that he is a rich tax collector. . . . "How can you tell?" you ask. . . . "First, he was scorned by the crowd. . . . Tax collectors are not very popular," Judas explains to you, "And I know he's rich by his clothes . . . fine linen and purple in color, . . . the color worn by the rich.". . .

Jesus stops under the sycamore tree that Zacchaeus has climbed, . . . looks up at Zacchaeus and calls, ... "Zacchaeus, come down immediately. I must stay in your house today.". . . The crowd begins to murmur. . . . They do not like the fact that Jesus is talking to a sinner, . . . or planning to go to his house. . . . Jesus ignores the crowd as he watches Zacchaeus scramble down the tree. . . . The sight of the short, fat man in rich clothes with his head gear of purple and white cloth tumbling half off and falling over one eye, makes you and the disciples laugh. . . . Zacchaeus does not seem to pay attention to his appearance as he lands at Jesus' feet and looks up. . . . "Lord, here and now I give half my possessions to the poor," he blurts out. . . . Jesus smiles at him . . . and reaches out his hand to help him up. . . . They begin to walk toward Zacchaeus' house. . . . Zacchaeus never stops talking. . . . You and Peter are now walking behind them and can hear the conversation. . . . "He seems to mean what he says," Peter remarks to you . . . as both of you listen to the tax collector promise to share his riches with the poor. . . .

The courtyard of Zacchaeus' house is so beautiful that you and the disciples become silent. . . . Zacchaeus gushes all over

you in his excitement, . . . his short fat body bouncing everywhere. . . . He invites you to make yourselves comfortable in the
courtyard while he goes into the house to see to the meal prep-
arations. . . . He never stops talking. . . . You can still hear his excited voice inside the house giving orders to the servants. . . .

Judas and Peter walk around the courtyard taking in all the
luxury that surrounds them. . . . Peter looks toward Jesus and
smiles. . . . "I doubt if he will give all this up, once he stops to
think about it.". . . Jesus slowly smiles. . . . "You forget, Peter,
that his heart has been touched by God. . . . Today salvation has
come into this house. . . ."

Jesus turns to you and smiles. . . . He takes your hand,. . .
looks into your eyes and says, ... "Zacchaeus believes in my
teachings and now wants to change his life and grow closer to
me." Jesus squeezes your hand and asks you, . . . "Do you believe in what I have taught?. . . Would you like to grow closer to
me? . . . I will help you, you know.". . .

I will leave you alone with Jesus so that you can listen to him
and answer his question to you.

Prayer

Jesus, I want to grow close to you. I need your help to do this
because sometimes I give up, or forget all about you. I love you,
Jesus, and want to be your close friend. (Invite spontaneous
prayer.)

It is time to leave Jesus. . . . Say good-bye for now. . . . You can
always return to him here in the courtyard. . . . Begin to walk
away. . . . Open you eyes and come back into the room.

Journal Writing

It is time to write your experience with Jesus in your journals.
Also write down any thoughts that come to you. For these
thoughts are from the Holy Spirit.

Sharing

Would anyone like to share their experience with the class?
Do you have any thoughts about ways you can grow closer to
Jesus? (List them on the board and invite the class to write these

ways in their journals if they wish.) It is important to grow close to God. Why? Do we need help from others to do this? Why? Who can help us? How can they help us? A name for helping and encouraging others is "nurturing." What happens to a plant if it is not nurtured—given water, food, and sunlight? The same thing happens to our spirit if it is not nurtured like the plant, it will not grow but wither and die. We are going to see this for ourselves, by watching two plants.

Follow-up

(Before class buy two small plants of the same species and size.) Show the class the two plants. Name one: Zacchaeus. Have someone print a name tag and place it around the pot. Tell the class that they will nurture Zacchaeus by placing it in the sunlight and giving it food and water. When they come to class they will go over to Zacchaeus and admire and encourage it to grow. The second plant will be placed away from the sun and given very little water and everyone will ignore it.

Closing Prayer

Gather in a semi-circle around the Bible and candle. Bring Zacchaeus and place it in the center of the circle. Take the other plant and put it in a place where it will not get sunlight. Also bring a glass with some water in it. While someone in the class pours water on Zacchaeus another person reads: "Jesus, as we nourish Zacchaeus with life-giving Water, help us to nourish each other as we try to grow closer to you."

Close with a song.

Music

"Come to the Water" from *Wood Hath Hope* (NALR).

"Zacchaeus" by Miriam T. Winter (Vanguard Music Corporation).

The Widow Who Gave

Mark 12:41-44; Luke 21:1-4

Introduction

Besides giving "things" to others, what other ways can we give? (List the children's suggestions on the board.) Which of the suggestions on the board is the hardest to do? Why? When we give, how does it help others? How does giving make you feel? Why? Is giving to others important? Why?

We are going to be with Jesus in the Temple and hear what he has to say about giving.

Meditation

Close your eyes. . . . Take a deep breath . . . and relax. . . . Jesus and his disciples are resting. . . . They are seated near the Temple treasuries . . . or collection boxes. . . . You are sitting with them watching people toss coins into the treasuries. . . . The part of the Temple you are in is as large as a gym, . . . only it is all marble. . . . The pillars are of white marble . . . and are so tall you feel like a tiny ant as you lean against one. . . . John points to the gold vines that decorate the Temple. . . . "Those gold clusters are as large as a man," he tells you. . . . "They seem smaller because they are so high up.". . .

Today there are more visitors than usual. . . . It is the time of the Passover and people from all over have come to Jerusalem to celebrate this great feast. . . . Between the loud voices of people greeting each other and the constant clanging of coins being tossed into the treasuries, . . . it is hard to hear the person next to you. . . .

You are sitting next to Jesus and listening to Matthew and Judas argue about the amount of money each person is tossing into the treasury. . . . Matthew, a former tax collector, speaks with authority. . . . "After all, I should know," he keep telling Judas. . . . They watch a man approach the treasury and toss in coins. . . . "He could have given much more," Matthew remarks. . . . "Look at his clothes,. . .he's a man of great wealth.". . . You turn and look at Jesus to see if he agrees with Matthew. . . . Jesus is not paying attention. . . . He is watching a woman walk toward the treasury. . . . The coins she tosses in barely make a sound as they drop into the treasury. . . . "She is a poor widow," Jesus explains to you. . . . "She gave two mites . . . a penny," Matthew remarks. . . .

Jesus watches the woman turn and begin to walk away. . . . He begins to speak and the disciples draw close in order to hear him. . . . "This woman has thrown in more than all the people who threw money into the treasury, . . . All of them gave out of their abundance, . . . but she gave out of her need and has thrown in everything that she had, . . . all she had to live on.". . . No one speaks as they watch the poor widow disappear into the crowd. . . .

Jesus places his hand on yours. . . . "That was a very brave and generous act, wasn't it?" he asks. . . . He continues to watch the widow fade into the crowd. . . . "Her faith and trust in God has grown by being generous in small things." Jesus sighs. . . . He turns and looks into your eyes. . . . "Will you help me teach others to trust in my Father's care and love for them?". . . Jesus watches you and sees your willingness. . . . "I will teach you how to begin," Jesus says. . . . He is now smiling because he is happy that you are willing to start. . . .

"Do little things for others, . . . your family, . . . helping around the house cheerfully, . . . or helping your brothers and sisters with homework for example. . . . Help your neighbors, . . . especially the elderly.". . . Jesus places His arm around your shoulders and says, . . . "I will be there to help you if you call on me. . . . Will you try?" he asks you. . . . Jesus waits silently for your answer. . . .

I will give you time with Jesus so that you can respond to him and listen to him.

Prayer

Jesus, I know that you want me to help others, and do it cheerfully. Sometimes it is hard and I don't want to help around the house. Stay close to me, Jesus, because I want to learn how to give myself to others. (Invite spontaneous prayer.)

It is time to leave. . . . Say good-bye to Jesus. . . . Begin to walk away. . . . Open your eyes and come back into the room.

Journal Writing

In your journals write not only your experience with Jesus and his disciples, but also the thoughts that come to you about giving. Listen to the Holy Spirit teach you in your thoughts.

Sharing

Would anyone care to share their experience and thoughts with the class? What organizations reach out to the poor and elderly? Why are they important? What would happen if they didn't exist? Are there any elderly people in your neighborhood? How could you help them? What about your parents, brothers and sisters, do they need help? Is it hard to help them? Why? Jesus asked us to do it "cheerfully," didn't he? Why is that important?

Follow-up

(Prepare before class: a large tree branch secured in a pot; green and fall color leaves made out of construction paper—several for each person in the class; red apples, made out of construction paper—one for each person in class.) Tell the children that they are going to give life to the tree by attaching "giving leaves" to it. Each leaf represents your witnessing God's love through an act of giving. When they reach out to someone by an act of kindness, they will take a leaf, write their name on it, and attach it to the tree. For ideas call their attention to the list on the board. (Suggestion: when their tree is filled with leaves they can bring it to the altar at the Preparation of Gifts.)

Closing Prayer

(On the board write "Jesus, I promise to try to help others cheerfully.") Sit in a semi-circle around the Bible and candle. Give each child a construction paper apple and a magic marker. Tell them that the apple represents the fruit of the gifts God has already given them. And these gifts will now be shared with others. Have them copy the "Promise" you wrote on the board. On the other side they are to sign their name. Have them attach their apple to the "Giving Tree" as they sing a song.

Music

"Peace Prayer" from *A Dwelling Place* (NALR).

"Prayer of St. Francis" and "All That We Have" from *Young People's Glory and Praise* (NALR).

At The Last Supper

Mark 14:22–25; Luke 22:17–20; Matthew 26:26–29

Introduction

When we love someone we want to be with that person. Jesus loved his close friends, the disciples. He knew that he was about to leave them and that they would not understand. He wanted them to know that he would always be with them in a special way. And that is why he gave himself to them, and to us, in the Eucharist.

Let us go to the upper room in Jerusalem and join Jesus and his disciples for the Lord's last Passover meal.

Meditation

Close your eyes. . . . Take a deep breath . . . and relax. . . . The room you are in, is large. . . . The walls are made of stone. . . . They remind you of the cement sidewalks around your house. . . . Touch them and feel their rough coolness. . . . The room is lit by lanterns, the kind you might use when you go camping. . . . They hang all around the room giving a soft light, . . .and casting dancing shadows on the stone walls. . . . The aroma of roasted lamb and wine fill the room. . . . This is part of the food and drink used in the ritual Passover Meal. . . .

The murmur of voices draws your attention to a group of men seated on cushions around a low table. . . . A few women are pouring wine into cups on the table. . . . The first person you recognize is Peter. . . . He reminds you of your favorite uncle. . . . It is good to see someone you know and like, isn't it? . . . Walk over to the table. . . . Place your hand on Peter's shoulder to get his attention. . . . His garment is rough in texture, . . . not smooth like

63

your clothes. . . . He turns and his eyes show that he recognizes you. . . . He smiles,. . .calls you by name and takes your hand in his. . . . "Come join us," Peter tells you. . . . The other disciples tell you, "Yes, come and join us.". . . One of the women brings a plate and goblet for you. . . . She smiles and waits . . . to see where you are going to sit. . . .

Someone else calls your name. . . . Do you recognize the voice? . . . It is Jesus! . . . Turn to him. . . . See his smile of greeting. . . . "Come sit beside me," Jesus tells you. . . . John moves over and lets you share his cushion. . . . Take your place next to Jesus. . . . He puts his arm around you, . . . hugs you to himself, . . . and whispers in your ear,. . . "I'm glad you came to be with me.". . . Feel how good it is to have Jesus hug and welcome you. . . .

Jesus turns from you and takes a piece of bread off the large plate in front of him. . . . It doesn't look like regular bread. . . . It looks more like pita bread. . . . He tears off a piece, . . . turns to you and gives you the piece of bread. . . . Jesus tells you, "Take this and eat, for this is my body.". . . Feel Jesus' hand touch yours as he gives you the bread. . . . He is looking into your eyes with love. . . . Take the piece of bread and eat it. . . . It tastes a little like pita bread, doesn't it? . . . Jesus passes the bread to the others who in turn tear off a piece and pass it on to the next person. . . . Everyone is now eating the bread. . . . No one is talking. . . . They all look very serious, don't they? . . . Jesus now takes his cup of wine and prays a blessing over it. . . . He gives the cup to you. . . . Looking into your eyes he tells you, "This is my blood to be poured out for many.". . . Take the cup from Jesus. . . . Taste the wine. . . . What does it taste like?. . . Pass the cup of wine to John. . . . Watch John take a sip and then pass it to Peter. . . . Jesus touches your hand. . . . Turn to him and see his love for you written in his eyes. . . . He softly speaks your name and asks, "Do you love me?"

I will now give you quiet time to be with Jesus. . . . You don't have to say anything if you don't want to. It is important to be still and just listen and experience being near your Lord.

Closing Prayer

Thank you, Jesus, for loving me so much that you gave yourself to me in this special way. Even though it is hard for me to understand, I do believe that you come to me in this bread and wine, just as you promised. I know that you love me and that this Eucharist is your special sign of love for me. (Invite the children to pray out loud to Jesus.) It is time to go now. . . . Say good-bye to Jesus. . .and quietly leave. . . . You know that you can always return any time you wish. . . . Open your eyes and come back into the room. . . .

Journal Writing

What were your thoughts and feelings while you were with Jesus? Write these down in your journal. Write down any thoughts or feelings you had or have, no matter how insignificant you may think they are. This is how the Holy Spirit speaks to you.

Follow-up

Ask the class to sit in a semi-circle around the Bible and candle. Next to the Bible place a plate with a piece of bread on it and a goblet filled with grape juice.

Explain to the children that you would like them to experience a simple sharing of food and drink. Tell them that when the bread is passed to them they are to tear a piece off and pass it on to the next person. When the goblet is passed, they are to take a sip and pass it to the next person. All this is to be done in silence. **Teacher:** (Take the bread and say:) "Jesus asks us to share what we have with each other."

(When all have taken a piece of the bread, take the goblet and say:) "Sharing and remembering Jesus' words is what Jesus asks his followers to do."

After the last person has shared the goblet of grape juice sing a closing song appropriate for the occasion.

Music

"Friends All Gather 'Round," "His Banner Over Me Is Love," "Jesus, Jesus," "We Come to Your Table" from *Young People's Glory and Praise* (NALR).

In the Garden with Jesus

Matthew 26:36-46

Introduction

Are there times when you find it hard to obey your parents or teachers? Why do you trust your parents when they tell you to do something without questioning? Have you ever felt like questioning them? Why did or didn't you? Why do you think it is important to obey?

Throughout his life, Jesus always said that he came to do his Father's will. However, there was one time when Jesus found it difficult to obey. We are going to be with Jesus at this time.

Meditation

Close your eyes. . . . Take a deep breath . . . and relax. . . . You and the disciples are following Jesus as he leads you down the stone steps leading from the upper room where you have just finished celebrating the Passover Meal. . . . The clattering of your sandals on the steps is the only sound that breaks the heavy silence that now surrounds you. . . . Jesus' face is drawn. . . . His body sags slightly as if he is carrying a heavy burden. . . . Jesus is leading you out of the city to the Garden of Gethsemane. . . .

Jesus stops at the entrance to the Garden. . . . "Sit here while I go and pray," he says. . . . Then turning to Peter, James, John and you the Lord asks you to follow him. . . . Leading you farther into the garden, Jesus stops and turns to you. . . . "My soul is very sorrowful, even to death," he tells you. . . . Looking at Peter, James and John Jesus tells them, "Remain here, and watch with me.". . . Follow Jesus as he walks a little further into the garden. . . . Again the Lord stops. . . . His knees begin to bend, . . . and his whole body collapses face down onto the ground. . . .

His arms are outstretched before him. . . . A sob, . . . or is it a deep sigh, comes from within him. . . . His body begins to shudder. . . . Walk closer. . . . Place your hand on Jesus' shoulder to comfort him. . . . Feel his body shake. . . . Jesus begins to plead with His Father. . . . "My Father, if it be possible, let this suffering pass from me;". . . he groans and becomes silent. . . . Jesus continues his prayer, . . . "Nevertheless, not as I will, but as you will.". . . His body stiffens and then relaxes in silence. . . .

Jesus slowly lifts himself up . . . and rests his hand heavily on your shoulder for help. . . . Walking over to Peter, James and John he finds them asleep. . . . "So you could not watch with me one hour," Jesus whispers sadly. . . . Turning from them, Jesus goes back to continue his prayer. . . . "My Father, if this cup of suffering cannot pass unless I drink it, . . . your will be done," he prays. . . . Jesus' clothes and hair are damp with perspiration. . . . Jesus again rises and walks over to his disciples, . . . sees they are still asleep, . . . sighs, . . . and turns away. . . . This time his prayer is one of acceptance. . . . His body no longer shakes. . . .

Jesus lifts himself up and rests back on his heels. . . . Wet strands of hair stick to his forehead and cheeks. . . . His eyes are filled with sadness as he turns to look at you. . . . Jesus sees your grief-stricken face, . . . places his hand on yours and speaks. . . . "You see I have come to do my Father's will. . . . it is his will that I now suffer and die for the salvation of mankind. . . . And so, I must continue.". . . Raising himself to his feet, Jesus looks deep into your eyes and says, "I must go now.". . . He slowly turns from you . . . and begins to walk toward the entrance to the garden. . . . You see many torch lights and hear voices shouting outside the garden. . . . Stay with Jesus. . . . I will give you time to be with him in the moment of his decision . . . to obey his Father. . . .

Prayer

Jesus, . . . Jesus, . . . I love you. . . . Help me to follow your example of obedience. I will remember this time with you when I find it hard to obey. (Invite spontaneous prayer.)

It is time to leave Jesus, . . . even though you want to stay and support him. . . . Open your eyes . . . and come back into the room.

Journal Writing

It is time to write in your journals. Spend time with Jesus and ask him to help you.

Sharing

Does anyone wish to share their experience, thoughts and feelings with the class? Why did Jesus go up to Peter, James and John so many times? Throughout his life Jesus always obeyed his Father without question. But this time he pleaded with his Father to change his mind. Why? Why did Jesus finally accept his Father's will? Why is it important for you to know that Jesus pleaded with his Father to change his will? Are there times in your life when you ask your parents or teachers to change their minds? Can you give an example?

Follow-up

The follow-up for this meditation is to have the children seriously look at Jesus' example and apply it to their lives. Therefore, after the sharing time ask the class to sit in a semi-circle around the Bible and candle. Invite them to share with each other some ways they will try to follow Jesus' example of obedience. . . . Close with a song.

Music

"Abba, Father" from *Abba! Father!* (NALR)

"All That We Have" from *Young People's Glory and Praise* (NALR).

"Here I Am, Lord" from *Lord of Light* (NALR).

Peter's Sorrow

Luke 22:54-71; Matthew 26:57-75; Mark 14:49-72

Introduction

Have you ever had the experience of someone not telling you the truth? How did that person act? It is hard to be honest, especially if you know that by telling the truth you might get into trouble. From your experience, what occasions tempt people your age to be dishonest? (List them on the board.) What alibi, or dishonest reasons, do they use to escape from admitting the truth? People often regret being dishonest at a later time. This happened to Peter at the time Jesus was arrested. Although he loved Jesus very much, he was frightened at the events that were suddenly taking place. We are going to be with Peter at this time.

Meditation

Close your eyes. . . . Take a deep breath . . . and relax. . . . It is late at night. . . . You and Peter have just entered the courtyard of the high priest. . . . The guards who arrested Jesus while he was praying in the Garden of Gethsemane have taken Jesus to the house of the high priest. . . . You and Peter are not allowed to enter the house and are waiting in the courtyard outside. . . . It all seems like a bad dream, . . . like you will soon wake up. . . . Everything and everyone around you seems unreal. . . . Your heart is pounding . . . you are very frightened. . . .

"Let's wait by the fire," Peter mutters to you. . . . He leads you over to the fire that is in the middle of the courtyard. . . . Guards and servants are standing around it to keep warm. . . . You hear them talking about Jesus' arrest, but are too heartsick to listen. . . . A servant studies Peter and says, "This man also was with him.". . . . Peter looks at the servant and says, "Woman, I do not know him.". . . "But, Peter. . ." you begin to protest. . . . "Quiet!" Peter tells you. . . .

Another servant of the high priest joins you. . . . As he warms his hands by the fire he studies Peter. . . . Squinting his eyes to get a closer look, he finally says, ... "You also are one of them." Peter looks up . . . and for a minute seems to stare through the servant. . . . "Man, I am not!" he responds. . . . The guards begin to take notice of Peter. . . . They say nothing, . . . just stare at him. . . . Soon they become disinterested and continue to talk among themselves about the latest arrest. . . .

A servant walks up to the fire. . . . He is bringing the latest news about the trial that is going on inside. . . . You can't quite understand what he is saying,. . .and are tempted to ask. . . . The servant turns and looks at Peter. . . . He frowns,. . .turns to the guard and points to Peter. . . . "Certainly this man also was with him; for he is a Galilean.". . . Peter gets up,. . .looks at the servant and says,. . . "Man, I do not know what you are saying.". . . With that Peter leaves and you follow him. . . . One of the roosters in the courtyard begins to crow. . . . Peter suddenly stops, . . . looks toward the rooster, . . . and gasps. . . . His face becomes drained of all its color. . . .

Just as you are about to ask Peter what is wrong someone shouts, . . . "Let the prisoner pass!". . . Peter and you turn to see Jesus being lead away. . . . His hands are tied! . . . As he passes you, . . . he pauses for a split second and looks at Peter. . . . The guard pushes Jesus on. . . . "Get going, prisoner . . . get going.". . .

For a minute you think your heart is going to break, . . . it hurts so much. . . . You seem frozen to the spot. . . . A deep sob from Peter shifts your attention to him. . . . He is no longer standing beside you, . . . but running out of the courtyard. . . . You try to follow him, . . . but he quickly disappears down a dark narrow street. . . . Before you can think of what to do next, . . . someone comes out of the shadows and walks up to you. . . . It is John. . . . "Come," he tells you and places his arm around your shoulders. . . .

You bury your head on his shoulder and begin to cry. . . . "Peter denied he knew Jesus . . . and I kept silent," you sob. . . . A feeling of uneasiness now begins to come over you. . . . "What should I do, John?" you whisper into his ear. . . . John stops walking, . . . rests his cheek on your head and says, "The Lord loves you, he forgives you!". . . Don't you remember what Jesus said only a few hours ago at the Passover Meal? . . . "This is my blood of the new covenant which is poured out for many for the FORGIVENESS of sins."?

John now begins to walk faster. . . . "Come, let us see if we can stay close to Jesus. . . . He needs our support now.". . . For a moment John's eyes meet yours, . . . his face is filled with kindness and understanding. . . . "Yes, sometimes it is hard to tell the truth. . . . Look what is happening to Jesus for telling the truth.". . .

I will give you time to be with John and talk to him about what he just said.

Prayer

Jesus, give me the courage to be an honest person. I love you and want to follow your teachings. (Invite spontaneous prayer.)

It is time to leave. . . . Say good-bye to John and begin to walk away. . . . Open your eyes . . . and come back into the room.

Journal

Write down your experiences, feelings and any thoughts that you have about telling the truth.

Sharing

How do you think Peter felt about himself after he denied that he knew Jesus? Why did he deny that he knew him? Would it have taken courage to admit the truth? Why? In your own life, does it sometimes take courage to admit the truth about something? Why?

Follow-up

The list on the board gives us situations in which we might be tempted to be dishonest. We are going to act out some of these situations. (This is an excellent opportunity to use puppets.) One person will be the one caught "in the act of" doing something wrong (fighting, skipping school or homework, etc.) The other person will be the one who catches him "in the act." The one caught will start excusing himself and then eventually tell the truth.

Closing Prayer

Gather around the Bible and candle, and sing an appropriate song.

Music

"Jesus, Jesus" and "Pardon Your People" from *Young People's Glory and Praise* (NALR).

"Hosea" from *Listen* (NALR).

Do You Love Me, Peter?

John 21:15-19

Introduction

Sometimes it is very hard to forgive someone who has turned against us. We are hurt. Peter hurt Jesus because he denied that he even knew Jesus when he was arrested. However, the Lord taught us to forgive others just as he forgave Peter for being disloyal. We are going to the Sea of Tiberias to be with Jesus as he forgives Peter.

Meditation

Close your eyes. . . . Take a deep breath . . . and relax. . . . You are sitting on a rock near a large body of water. . . . There is sand along the edge of the water. . . . It is a beach. . . . Dig your feet into the sand to keep them warm. . . . It is cool on the beach so early in the morning. . . . The sun is just beginning to rise. . . . Look at all the beautiful colors the sun's rays make on the few clouds in the sky. . . . There are oranges and yellows and golds. . . . Even the whitecaps on the gentle rolling waves moving onto the shore have touches of sparkling gold on them. . . .

Feel the freshness of the sea's air. . . . Take a deep breath and let the cool air go deep into your lungs. . . . Look around you. . . . What do you see? . . . What do you hear? . . . Do you hear the cry of those large white and grey birds called seagulls? . . . Watch them as they swoop over the sea looking for fish. . . .

Notice that there is a fishing boat not too far from shore. . . . You can hear the faint murmurs of the voices of the fishermen. . . . They seem excited. . . . It looks as though they have a large catch of fish, doesn't it? . . . They are struggling with their nets. . . .

There is someone standing on the beach. . . . It is hard to see him clearly, because the sun hasn't cast enough light yet. . . . Walk over to him. . . . He is also watching the fishermen. . . . You try to hurry but your feet sink into the sand and makes walking difficult. . . .

As you approach, the man turns to you. . . . He smiles because he recognizes you. . . . Do you know him? . . . It is Jesus! . . . He calls you by name and invites you to join him. . . . Jesus places his arm around your shoulders and the two of you walk along the shore toward a campfire on the beach. . . . It is good to be with Jesus, isn't it? . . . It is good to be alone with him, . . . standing by the camp-fire. . . . Jesus tells you that he is preparing a breakfast for his friends. . . . Look into the orange and blue flames and see the fish cooking. . . .

Someone joins you. . . . It is Peter. . . . His clothes are all wet and he is breathing hard. . . . He was so anxious to see Jesus that he dove into the water from the boat and swam to shore. . . . Jesus looks at Peter. . . . "Come," the Lord tells Peter and you, as he places his arms around your shoulders and leads you down the beach away from the others who are now coming to shore. . . .

Jesus stops . . . and turns to Peter. . . . "Simon, son of John, do you truly love me?" Jesus asks him. . . . Study Peter's face. . . . See the tears begin to fill his eyes. . . . His voice chokes as he answers. . . . "Yes Lord," Peter says, "you know that I love you." Jesus tells him, "Feed my lambs.". . . Again Jesus asks Peter, "Simon, son of John, do you truly love me?" Peter looks at Jesus with a pleading expression in his eyes and answers, "Yes, Lord, you know that I love you." Jesus tells him, "Take care of my sheep.". . . Jesus asks Peter a third time, "Simon, son of John, do you love me?" Peter looks hurt, . . . but he answers Jesus, "Lord, you know all things, you know that I love you." And Jesus again tells Peter, "Feed my sheep.". . . You wonder why Jesus is asking Peter so many times. . . . Do you think it is because Peter denied Jesus three times? . . . Jesus turns to you. . . . His eyes seem to look into your very soul. . . . He places his hand on your shoulder, . . . speaks your name, . . . and asks you, . . . "Do you love me?"

Silence Time

I will leave you with Jesus so that you can answer him. Remember to listen to what Jesus tells you.

Closing Prayer

Jesus, I do love you. I want to be a loyal friend to you like you are to me. Teach me how to be loyal and to forgive my friends when they hurt me. (Invite the children to pray aloud.)

It is time to leave Jesus. . . . Say good-bye, . . .and begin to leave. . . . Turn and wave good-bye. . . . Open your eyes. . .and come back into the room. . . .

Journal Writing

What thoughts do you have on being loyal to your friends and forgiving them when they hurt you? Write these thoughts down. Write down any experience you had while you were with Jesus.

Sharing Time

Do you have any thoughts on forgiveness and loyalty that you would like to share with the class? When you forgive someone, is it hard to forget what they did to you? Is it hard to forget something you did for which you were sorry? Were you aware of what you did when you hurt someone? If you knew just how much you hurt that person would you have done it?

Follow-up

It is very hard to forgive ourselves for something we did. We have already been forgiven by Jesus, but do we believe it? I want you to imagine what Jesus would say as he forgives you. Pretend you are Jesus who is writing a letter to you. Have Jesus forgive you for something you did and tell you why he has forgiven you. If you do not know what to say, ask Jesus to help you. (Suggest to the class that they put this letter in their journals.)

Music

"Jesus, Jesus" from *Young People's Glory and Praise* (NALR).

"Do You Really Love Me" from *Hi, God!* (NALR).

Jesus Sends the Spirit

Acts 2:1–13

Introduction

Have you ever been afraid? What are some of the things that people your age are afraid of? (List them on the board.) When you were little did you ever become frightened at night by a sound or a shadow in your room? Did you call out to your mother or father? How did you feel when they turned on the light in your room and came to your bedside to hug you? The Holy Spirit is like that loving, comforting parent—always with us, ready to shed light on our problems, ready to calm our fears.

You remember that after Jesus died on the cross and rose from the dead, he came back to see his family and friends. He visited the apostles and assured them that he was alive. It was so comforting to be with Jesus again. Then one day he went back to heaven. The apostles felt alone. They were also afraid that they would be arrested by the same people that put Jesus to death. In fact, they even hid in the upper room. I imagine that when they left the room they would sneak out quickly, looking left and right to make sure they weren't being followed. However, Jesus knew their fears, and before he ascended into heaven he promised that he would send them a special Helper, the Holy Spirit. He told them to stay in the city until the Holy Spirit came to them. They would know Him because he would be in them (John 14:16, 17).

We are going to the upper room in the city of Jerusalem and experience with the apostles the coming of the Holy Spirit on the first Pentecost.

Meditation

Close your eyes. . . . Take a deep breath . . . and relax. You are in the upper room. . . . It is crowded with people. . . . A few small windows let a little light in. . . . Lanterns, like the ones you might use when going camping, are hung around the room. . . . Their flickering flames cast dancing shadows on the stone walls. . . .

It is stuffy and warm in the room. . . . And to make matters worse, . . . there are about 120 people here today. . . . The door to the room is closed and locked. . . . If it were open there would be more air. . . . No one seems to notice how uncomfortable it is here. . . .

Mary, Jesus' mother, is sitting in a corner of the room. . . . People are gathered around and talking to her. . . . Suddenly, there is a knock on the door. . . . Everyone in the room stops talking and anxiously looks toward the door. . . . Peter walks over, leans his head against the door and whispers, . . . "Who is it?". . . The man on the other side identifies himself. . . . Peter relaxes, and quickly opens the door. . . . Philip slips inside the room. . . . Feel the tension leave the room. . . . Conversation begins again. . . . John sees the puzzled look on your face. . . . He walks over to you and explains. . . . "We have to be careful, because those who arrested Jesus might be looking to arrest us.". . .

As John is speaking, . . . a sound like the blowing of a violent wind suddenly fills the room. . . . Then, what seems to be tongues of fire appear over the heads of everyone, . . . even you. . . . A peace begins to flow through you. . . . It is followed by a feeling of joy that you never before experienced. . . . It fills your whole mind and body. . . . Let these feelings flow through you. . . . Enjoy them. . . .

Peter begins to shout, "The power of the Holy Spirit is upon us, . . . just as Jesus promised!". . . He begins to clap his hands and laugh with joy. . . . His face glows with happiness . . . and he begins to sing praise to God. . . . Someone starts a circle dance . . . and others join in. . . . John grabs your hand and the two of you join in the dance. . . . The circle goes faster and faster, . . . more and more people join the circle. . . . Everyone is singing and laughing. . . . You feel lighthearted and joyful. . . .

Suddenly, Peter breaks away from the circle and dashes to the door. . . . He flings it open and rushes outside. . . . You can hear his voice praising God as he runs. . . . A crowd is beginning to gather outside; they have heard the strange sounds of wind coming from the upper room. . . . Peter begins to tell them about Jesus. . . . The other apostles follow Peter while the rest of you continue to dance and sing. . . . You are beginning to experience not only a joy but also a courage that helps you express your happiness without being embarrassed. . . . Now, a feeling of love for others fills your heart. . . . You want to be next to them and tell them that you like them. . . . I am going to leave you so that you can continue to experience the first Pentecost with all of your new friends.

Prayer

Come, Holy Spirit, we open our hearts to your love. Fill us with your joy and courage. Help us to want to tell others about you and to bring your peace and joy to them. We praise you and thank you. (Lead the class into spontaneous prayer.)

It is time to leave. . . . Say good-bye to Mary . . . and to all your new friends. . . . See their joy-filled faces as they say good-bye and invite you to come back and join them. . . . Open your eyes . . . and come back into the room.

Journal Writing

Write down the experiences and feelings you had while you were in the upper room. Ask the Holy Spirit to help you. Write any thoughts you have no matter how insignificant they might seem to you. Learn to respect the thoughts you have while in prayer. You are being inspired by the Holy Spirit.

Sharing

Is there anyone who would like to share their experience with the class? (The children can be lead to understand that the Holy Spirit often speaks to us through other people.)

Follow-up

Prepare before class a piece of paper for each child. At the top of the paper put a picture of a dove—symbol of the Holy Spirit, and the words, "The Holy Spirit and Me." (Red ink will make this more dramatic.)

Tell the class: This week let's see if we can be aware of the guidance of the Holy Spirit in our lives. I am going to give each of you a piece of paper. Place it near your bed tonight. Each night before you go to sleep, ask the Holy Spirit to help you see how he has helped you that day. Write your thoughts on your special piece of paper. Next week bring your paper back to place in your journal. Those who wish will share their experience with the class.

Closing Prayer

Gather in a circle around the Bible and candle. Join hands and say a prayer to the Holy Spirit. Invite a spontaneous prayer. Close with a song to the Holy Spirit.

Music

"Everyone Moved by the Spirit," "The Spirit is A-Movin' " and "Spirit, Move" from *Young People's Glory and Praise* (NALR).

"Lord, Send Out Your Spirit" from *Path of Life* (NALR).

Index A: Biblical Passages

Numbers given in parenthesis refer to the meditation number, not the page number.

Index B: Human Experience Symbols

Index C: Gospel Images

Numbers given refer to the meditation number, not the page number.